W9-AEL-794

THE NEW JERUSALEM
IN THE REVELATION OF JOHN

GRACE LIBRARY CARLOW COLLEGL
PITTSBURGH PA 15213

The New Jerusalem in the Revelation of John

The City as Symbol of Life with God

Bruce J. Malina

BS
2825.6
J4
M35
2000
C. 2

A Michael Glazier Book
THE LITURGICAL PRESS
Collegeville, Minnesota

CATALOGUED

Zacchaeus Studies: New Testament

General Editor: Mary Ann Getty

A Michael Glazier Book published by The Liturgical Press

Cover design by David Manahan, O.S.B. Illustration: Der Verduner Altar, detail: *The Heavenly Jerusalem,* 14th cent., Klosterneuburg, Austria.

Figure 1 in this book, from *On the Message and Genre of Revelation* by Bruce J. Malina, is reprinted with permission of Hendrickson Publishers © 1995.

Quotations of the book of Revelation are the author's translation.

© 2000 by The Order of St. Benedict, Inc., Collegeville, Minnesota. All rights reserved. No part of this work may be reproduced or transmitted in any form or by any means, electronic or mechanical, including photocopying and record-ing, or by any information storage or retrieval system without the prior written permission of The Liturgical Press unless such copying is expressly permitted by federal copyright law. Address inquiries to: Permissions, The Liturgical Press, Collegeville, MN 56321. Printed in the United States of America.

1   2   3   4   5   6   7   8

Library of Congress Cataloging-in-Publication Data

Malina, Bruce J.
    The new Jerusalem in the revelation of John : the city as symbol of life with God / Bruce J. Malina.
        p.   cm. — (Zacchaeus studies. New Testament)
    Includes bibliographical references.
    ISBN 0-8146-5938-1 (alk. paper)
    1. Jerusalem in the Bible.   2. Bible. N.T. Revelation XXI–XXII—Socio-rhetorical criticism.   3. Cities and towns, Ancient—Mediterranean Region.   4. Astronomy in the Bible.   I. Title.   II. Series.

BS2825.6.J4 M35   2000
228'.06—dc21
                                                                00-021133

For my Palestinian sons,
Musa and Said Al Hindi,
who look forward to the coming of the New Jerusalem

GIFT OF MARY ANN GETTY-SULLIVAN 4-27-04

Contents

List of Figures

Preface

The subject of this brief volume is the concluding vision of the book of Revelation. What it offers are reading scenarios describing and explaining the two major entities at the close of the book: the celestial city and the cosmic Lamb. The "marriage" of these two marks the highlight of John's presentation.

Research into this New Testament document has produced an endless supply of studies (see the recent annotated bibliography by Muse 1996). There is little doubt that the most complete, rather encyclopedic study of the book of Revelation is the three-volume commentary of David E. Aune (1997–1999). Yet this commentary, along with recent specialized studies of the celestial city in Revelation (e.g., Sim 1996; Stander 1998), simply presumes that modern readers know what an ancient city meant to those who lived in them or were affected by them. Even those who have described and analyzed those first "urban" members of Jesus-groups never define what "city" meant in the past. The presumption seems to be that ancient cities, to a large extent, were like modern cities minus modern technology (steam engine, electricity, internal combustion engine, etc.).

It is not the purpose of the present study to supply the wealth of information that traditional works provide. The reader looking for details of interest can only benefit by having recourse to those works. Rather, the aim of this book is to delineate a comparative model for understanding the meaning of a city in antiquity. What was the type of city described by John, and what would the marriage of such a celestial city mean to first-century Mediterraneans? The definition and comparative model of the city presented here should prove equally useful for persons interested in understanding those first "urban" members of Jesus-groups addressed by other New Testament documents.

Bruce J. Malina

1

Presuppositions About Language and Reading

The author of the book of Revelation was a Jesus-group prophet named John. As is well known from the literary study of the book of Revelation, the first three verses of the work trace back to a compiler or editor who took John's letter to the seven Asian churches and inserted four of John's major visions into that letter. This compiler himself considered John the seer to be a prophet in the Jesus tradition (Rev 1:1-3). In perhaps the very first interpretation of the genre of the book, this compiler labeled the set of visions that John offered his readers/hearers an *apokalypsis*. This Greek word means "revelation," the making known of something about persons previously not known (Smith 1983).

John's description of the final vision of the book begins as follows: "And I saw the holy city [*polis*], the new Jerusalem, coming down out of the sky from God, prepared as a bride adorned for her husband" (21:2). How does one come to understand what John the prophet is talking about? What sort of city descends from the sky? What sort of city gets married? Why would any city be called "holy"? While the usual translation of the Greek word *polis* is "city," how many modern Bible readers have the experience of a "city" that matches anything like what was called a *polis* in antiquity? Why is the celestial city called "new Jerusalem"? And why is this vision of the holy city descending from the sky preceded by the author's initial observation: "Then I saw a new sky and a new land: for the first sky and the first land had passed away and the sea was no more" (21:1)? What steps must one take to interpret such statements?

1. Expectations and Perceptions

Consider the following incident, which has nothing directly to do with biblical studies but which has much to say about interpretation, including biblical interpretation. The story illustrates how presumptions based on one's own preconceptions and lack of awareness of what others mean in their own social setting (or for Bible readers, in their own culture) may affect a scholar's perception. Twenty years ago D. L. Rosenhan, a psychologist at Stanford University, directed the following experiment:

> Eight sane people gained secret admission to twelve different hospitals located in five different states on the East and West coasts. The quality of the hospitals varied from old and shabby ones to quite new research-oriented and well-staffed ones. All but one were supported by federal, state, or university funds. One of the eight pseudopatients was a psychology student in his twenties. The other seven were older and "established": three psychologists, a pediatrician, a psychiatrist, a painter, and a housewife. Except for alleging hallucinatory symptoms to gain admission and falsifying name, vocation, and employment to avoid identification, no further alterations of person, history, or circumstances were made. Upon entering the psychiatric ward, each pseudopatient "ceased simulating any symptoms of abnormality" (Rosenhan 1973: 251). In spite of their show of sane behavior in the ward, in eleven of the twelve admissions, the experimenters were each diagnosed as "schizophrenic." In one admission that pseudopatient was diagnosed as "manic depressive." The perceptions of hospital staff, including psychiatrists, were so controlled by the psychiatric setting and by what

they expected that they failed to differentiate any of the pseudo-patients from the real patients (Rosenhan 1973: 250–258; cited from Hsu 1983: 426).

Obviously the foregoing experiment indicates the significant point that preconceptions and context color both the expectations and the perceptions that emerge in a person's interpretation of a social situation. Readers always bring expectations and perceptions to their reading, whether it be of newspapers or college textbooks. What do readers expect to find in the book of Revelation? How do they perceive what they are reading? If Bibles were kept exclusively in hospitals, would not Bible readers believe that the books have to do with healing? And what if all phone books were the exclusive property of churches, with each person bringing his or her own phone book to church on Sunday? Would we not believe that phone books were religious documents? Would not religious scholars proceed to develop a sort of magical onomatographical and numerological hermeneutic of the phone books in question? Impossible, you might say, except on *Star Trek* and its successors! Or is it really impossible?

The modern scholarly study of the book of Revelation is much concerned with how preconceptions and cultural context color expectations and perceptions. A first and fundamental step in filtering out modern American expectations and perceptions is to determine what kind of document the book of Revelation is. What we expect to find in this book depends entirely on the kind of writing we think it is. The reason for this is that we interpret our experiences, including our experiences of types of speech or types of writing, on the basis of the social contexts with which we are acquainted. All the social contexts available to us derive from and constitute the social system into which we have been enculturated (see Malina 1982; 1983).

2. Meaning and Social System

Meanings in spoken and written patterns derive from social systems. For example, if one were to see a newspaper advertisement stating "T-bone Steaks, $4.00 per pound," no U.S. person would think it is a movie advertisement giving the title of the film and cost of admission but would recognize it is a food advertisement. Food advertisements are a subtype of advertisements. Advertisements are common in social systems with a market-based economy. The food advertisement cited above is a shorthand notice for: "The cut of beef known as T-bone steak can be purchased this week (only) for $4.00 (U.S.) per pound in the food market placing this advertisement in this newspaper (or flyer)." As an abbreviated notice, such advertisements are high-context statements. They do not articulate all the dimensions of what one would have to explain to, say, a Hindu villager who never left India.

Food advertisements make sense to their readers because there are, in fact, food markets that they have experienced, and eating beef is customary. Such food advertisements express a complete thought. In this they are like sentences, groups of words expressing a complete thought. As a rule, sentences do not express complete meanings. Consider the sentence "He did so." This sentence is a complete thought but has no interpretable meaning without its presumed context. At times it takes thousands of sentences (complete thoughts) to communicate a simple meaning. A good example of this is a philosophical treatise dealing with time or being. The point is that the unit of meaning in language, both in newspapers and in the Bible, is not the sentence; rather, the unit of meaning is the spoken or written type of language pattern embedded in the social system, that is, the genre. Similarly, the individual advertisement statement ("T-bone Steaks, $4.00 per pound") does not express a complete meaning without some presumed written type of language pattern (advertisement) that realizes a dimension of the social system.

All spoken and written patterns of language derive their meaning from some social system. These spoken and written patterns are often quaintly called "literary forms," although they have nothing directly to do with literature or anything literary. They are types of language patterns used for realizing meanings from a social system in speech or in writing. We learn to expect a range of meanings to be communicated in language on the basis of types of language patterns people use to speak or write.

What this means for reading a document such as the book of Revelation is that in order to be considerate readers, we must bring to our reading an understanding of the social system of the author. Normally communication takes place the other way around: we expect people who communicate with us (such as teachers, writers, TV announcers) to be considerate by taking us, the audience, into account. We expect them to communicate with us, to speak "on the same wavelength," that is, in terms of our shared social system. In such a case mutual understanding is highly probable. Our social system provides us with sets of typical scenarios embracing a range of experiences by means of which we can imagine what other people in the same system are talking about. If we do not share the same scenarios with a particular speaker or writer, then we either do not understand or we misunderstand what they are trying to say and mean.

Such non-understanding and misunderstanding have usually been the case with John's Revelation. If a reader cannot figure out what some writer says and means to say, and if the writing is very important (a sacred scripture), then the reader will apply inappropriate references outside the historical period and outside the social context of the author to interpret what the author speaks about. Applying inappropriate references to interpret an author's statements outside the author's historical period is called *anachronism* (for example: if Jesus traveled in Palestine, he must have had a jeep). Applying inappropriate references to interpret what an author says outside the author's social context is called *ethnocentrism* (for example: Jesus condemned divorce; we have divorce in our society, so Jesus must be condemning our type of divorce).

As is well known, the book of Revelation has been subject to endless anachronistic and ethnocentric interpretations. Even though first-century Mediterraneans lived in a ruralized, peasant society, characterized by a present-time orientation, readers find endless reference to the distant future (even the twentieth and twenty-first centuries) in this book. This is extreme anachronism, in face of the fact that John tells of "what must soon take place" (1:1 and 22:6).

First-century Mediterraneans had no functioning abstract future category at all; rather, they had a present-based future that we might call the forthcoming—a future based on what exists in the present (see Malina 1996b). For example, if a woman is pregnant, one can predict she will have a baby, perhaps even nine months from now. If a farmer plants a field in the spring, one can predict that plants will soon sprout in the field. And if a football game begins, one can predict at the opening of the first quarter that a fourth quarter will follow. And given what John the prophet has seen in his vision, all will take place "soon." Yet the Bible consists of countless "predictions" of the forthcoming, many of which never occurred (for example, Luke 9:27: "But truly I tell you, there are some standing here who will not taste death before they see the kingdom of God"; or Matthew 10:23: "For truly I tell you, you will not have gone through all the towns of Israel before the Son of Man comes."

Now if the book of Revelation describes only the author's present and what is forthcoming soon on the basis of that present, how do so many people find references to the future in that book? Of course, the answer is that they dismiss the author and the original audience as insignificant and presume that the book speaks directly to them and their times. Theologically, such readers do not really believe in an inspired biblical author but in an inspired biblical reader (see Malina 1991). Whatever meaning they might come up with is the meaning intended by the God who is inspiring them in their reading. Such readings are often allegorical (referring to something other than the person, object, time, or place to which the author refers).

At other times, even historically oriented scholars, searching for meanings in the author's historical setting, come up with messages relevant to our contemporary world, for example a message of justice and an end to oppression today (see Wengst 1994). These scholars justify their approach in terms of aesthetic principles developed by devotees of literary fiction in the Romanticism of the nineteenth century and much alive today in the guise of "Post-Modern" literary criticism (see Prickett 1996). In this perspective "a text has a life of its own," and whatever meanings a reader derives from a "text" is as valid as the meanings any other readers might propose. While this may work for the so-called New

Criticism and Post-Modernism, it is totally silly in social life. Even such critics do not believe that "texts" such as a restaurant bill or a summons to court or a contract to buy a house has a life of its own!

Biblical scholarship is ultimately rooted in the reading of ancient written documents, and therefore in the interpretation of written language. Written language does not live in scrolls or books; rather, the markings on a page stand for or represent wordings that represent meanings that can come alive only through the agency of the minds of readers. Quite emphatically, "texts" do not have a life of their own! It is readers who give life to the writings they read. As a readership changes, the meanings realized in writings can change, especially if the readership consists of inconsiderate readers, unconcerned with what the original author might wish to say and mean to the original audience.

3. About Language

Readers, as a rule, have some preconceptions about how language works. Most do not reflect on the fact that language is a three-tiered affair. Readers in a given social system come to understand the meanings of their social system as imparted by authors of some document through wordings made concrete in the markings of a writing system. While our acquaintance with the markings of writing systems (orthography) and the patterns of wording systems (lexico-grammar and syntax) has required many years of elementary and high school study, the meanings expressed in language patterns and markings always derive from a social system (see Halliday 1978).

Many U.S. persons study foreign languages. As a rule, foreign-language study consists of learning to write and/or spell words of the foreign language (orthography) as well as mastering vocabulary, sentence formation, conversation, and the like (lexico-grammar and syntax). Unless the U.S. language-learner knows the social system of the persons who are native speakers and writers of the foreign language in question, what the U.S. person learns is how to speak English in German, French, or Japanese. Thus if U.S. persons read the book of Revelation in the original Greek without knowledge of the social system of the author who expressed social-system meanings through Greek wordings and spellings, they will necessarily come up with meanings based in the U.S. social system.

The point, in sum, is that language is a three-level affair: meanings from a social system are realized through wordings which, in turn, are realized through concrete markings or sounds. These distinctions are known even to non-literate persons who realize that they can change wordings (make it stronger? not so harsh?) and still come up with the same meaning. In all language communication, readers and hearers inevitably bring their knowledge of some social system(s) to their linguistic interaction. Since documents of the past come alive only in the mind of readers, how, in fact, does reading work?

4. About Reading: Literate Misconceptions

The first procedure that biblical interpreters, professional and non-professional, apply in their pursuit of understanding a biblical document is reading. Most biblical interpreters are unaware of what reading actually entails. Empirical studies of the reading process indicate that when literate people reflect upon what they think they are doing when they read, what they describe is actually quite off target (see Malina 1996a; for what follows, see Sanford and Garrod 1981).

People who know how to read and write usually think that what they read is what they call a "text." By "text" they mean an instance of written language that has the shape of a sort of super-sentence. This, of course, is a logical perspective for those whose training in language focused on wording, that is, the sentence- and word-level of a writing. In this view, the "text" being read evokes mental representations or ideas in the mind of the reader. These, in turn, consist of a chain or series of statements or propositions that derive directly from the chain of sentences that constitute the "text," which is made up of sentences, which in turn are made up of words. The reader basically performs two tasks: parsing the "text" into propositional units, and then connecting the resulting propositions in some way. This connection takes place by means of some superstructure embedded in language itself. Such superstructures are called variously deep structures, story grammars, narrative grammars, or something of the sort. As most will recognize, this sort of model undergirds contemporary structuralism and most literary-critical exegesis. The difficulty with the model is that it cannot be verified experimentally. Indeed, the research of experimental psychologists indicates that this is not what goes on in the mind of a reader at all.

Such a conceptual approach to language is rooted in presuppositions about the nature and function of language that derive from the reification of highly abstract entities like words and sentences. To "reify" is to "thingify," that is, to consider abstract entities as though they were concrete things. In this case, literate people tend to think that words and sentences are rather concrete things. After all, do not dictionaries consist of lists of words, and cannot one see written sentences marked off by punctuation when one reads? The difficulty is that the partitioning of language into words and sentences is a highly abstract, arbitrary process, understood only by the literate. When people speak, there is no separation between words and sentences such as those devised for concretizing language in the arbitrary squiggles of writing.

Furthermore, words and sentences are not the end-products of language. The end-products of language are meanings. More specifically, these end-products are spoken and/or written meaningful configurations of language intended to communicate, such as the food advertisement mentioned above. Such configurations are culturally significant types of spoken and written language. Adult native speakers of a language know literally hundreds of types of spoken and written language, such as greetings, jokes, directions given to others, news broadcasts, speeches, and so on. Types of written language include books of various types, newspapers and their many subtypes, "Dear Occupant" letters, bills, and such. Language mediates meaning. And as noted above, written documents, like coherent speech, invariably communicate meaning that derives from, and forms part and parcel of, some social system.

Those abstract entities we call words and sentences are the means for realizing meaning; they are wording or ways of linguistic communication at an analytic level. The human ability to communicate is the ability to mean. Language is used to convey meaning (although not all meaning is "languaging"). The unit of meaning (not of thought) is some type of patterned writing or speaking, that is, a linguistic form or genre such as those previously mentioned. In spite of the fact that literate persons produce mounds of notes from their readings, those notes (a chain or series of propositions or sentences) are not what reading evokes in the mind of a reader. How, then, does reading work?

5. How Reading Works

The explanation of the reading process that has been verified by experimental psychologists might be called a scenario model. This model considers a written document as the written expression of a succession of explicit and implicit scenes or schemes in which the mental representation evoked in the mind of the reader consists of a series of settings, episodes, or models deriving directly from the mind of the reader, coupled with appropriate alterations to these settings, episodes, or models as directed by what the author of the written document says. Here, too, the reader must perform two tasks: s/he has to use what is stated in the writing to identify an appropriate "domain of reference," that is, call to mind an appropriate scene, scheme, or model as suggested by the document, and then s/he must use the identified "domain of reference" as the larger frame within which to situate the meanings proposed in the writing as far as this is possible. In this case, an author must have his or her readers in mind so that both might share a common social domain of reference and sets of scenarios allowing for the communication of meaning.

What this means is that if contemporary persons are to be considerate readers of ancient documents, they must equip themselves with appropriate scenarios rooted in the social systems of the authors whose writings they intend to read. Otherwise the outcome of the reading process can only be misunderstanding or non-understanding. Consequently, it would seem that the best preparation that a contemporary reader of the Bible can acquire is a set of scenarios deriving from, and appropriate to, the social system from which the biblical books derive and thus facilitate biblical understanding. The understanding and interpretation of any sort of writing is ultimately rooted in a social system along with a set of scenarios sketching how the world of the author works. All interpretation, it would seem, requires such scenarios and ultimately rests on them.

6. Considerate Reading: Scenarios and Models

The scenarios we bring to reading a document or to "reading" some social interaction is a sort of model. A model is the outcome of human abstract thinking (see Carney 1975: 1–46). Human beings cannot keep more than seven, plus or minus two, disparate items in mind at once. Those humans who go on to abstract thinking after puberty inevitably conjure up models (for example, of food, clothing, CDs, cars, etc.) in order to handle the multiple and disparate information with which they are bombarded. A model is an abstract, simplified representation of some real-world object that human beings develop in order to understand, control, and predict. To envision the social system of any human group, one must think in terms of a sort of model that offers categories of human experience and behavior that serve to help understand, control, and predict the flow of human interaction.

Such models of human interactions are social science models— models from sociology (for one's own society), from social and cultural anthropology (for comparison of two or more societies), and social-psychology (for dealing with individuals in their respective societies). Social science models are models of the systems of the interactions, structures, and functions of people in groups. The models describe processes of interaction or organized patterns of collective behavior. The understanding and interpretation of human behavior is always based on models of how social interaction works, whether the person interpreting is aware of the model (explicit models) or unaware (implicit models), since human beings make abstractions in order to understand.

2

The Genre of the Book of Revelation

Scholarly biblical interpretation, like the scholarly interpretation of any written language, is based upon, and derives from, scenarios or models of how the world of human beings works (social sciences) and models of the nature and function of language (sociolinguistics). However, most interpreters will agree that the biblical documents that they are to interpret are writings from the past. They are not simply foreign language works from a contemporary, socially different group of people (for example, like today's newspapers from Cairo or Berlin), but documents from a non-contemporary social group. Hence some sort of historical models are equally required. What, then, is the relationship between history and the social sciences that provide scenarios from other societies?

Social sciences are based upon models of how the world of human interaction works and why it works that way. Specifically, the social sciences look to how meanings are socially imposed on men and women in order to explain human behavior in terms of typicalities. They underscore generalities, the common elements of meaning typical of a given social group. On the borderline between the social sciences and the humanities is that set of models called history. History focuses upon the "that," "how," and "why" human beings created meanings in the past that affect our present with a view to our future. History, with its roots in the present and a set of working images of the past, seeks to explain events in terms of the distinctiveness of agents and agencies, in terms of particularities and differences. The other social sciences, rooted in the present, prescind from the past, for the most part, to seek out generalities, commonalities, samenesses.

The problem with history as a way of interpretation of alien meaning is that in order to ferret out distinctiveness, all the commonalities of the area under study have to be known and articulated. For example, to know the unique quality of the book of Revelation, one has to know about all the writings of the same type that existed in the first-century Mediterranean world.

> Nothing is apparently more exact and definite than the historian's habitual concentration on concrete detail. But this appearance of exactitude is deceptive. The idea that history is a series of self-explanatory concrete facts is an assumption of the same order as Dr. Johnson's proof of the reality of a chair by kicking it, or the refutation of the Copernican system by pointing out that anyone can see the sun moving across the skies from morning to night. The common-sense assumptions on which historians rely amount, in fact, to vague untested, unreliable generalizations, whose "validity is frequently not much greater than the explanations of physical events given by primitive tribes" [Bagby 1958: 37] . . . they fail to make their assumptions explicit and are unsystematic in their generalizations (Barraclough 1978: 58).

Historians, for the most part, have relied upon disciplined intuition alone (often sophisticated ethnocentrism) to account for commonalities. Parade examples of such sophisticated ethnocentrism can be found in the various attempts to determine the type of writing to which Revelation belonged on the basis of the types of writing known to persons in various contemporary university departments: fiction, description of visionary experiences, a tissue of Old Testament sentences and phrases (midrash), as though the first-century Mediterranean world was that of modern Northern Europe or North America.

Another vogue in historical interpretation is to consider the main problems of ancient peasant societies to be those of today's market system: political oppression and economic injustice. It comes as no surprise when interpreters of Revelation see the prophet dealing with these two problems in the first-century Mediterranean world, even though the social systems of the day did not focus on oppression and injustice. The value of outfitting the book of Revelation with one or more of the foregoing categories and concerns is that the document can still be said to have respectability and direct value for contemporary believers.

As fiction, the work would be an imaginary, symbolic narrative "in which a revelation is mediated by an otherworldly being to a human recipient, disclosing a transcendent reality which is both temporal, insofar as it envisages eschatological salvation, and spatial, insofar as it involves another, supernatural world" (Collins 1979: 9). Since the work deals with "eschatological salvation," the author would be inviting his readers to discern actual historical events that are forthcoming and mark the end of human existence on the planet as we know it. As a set of visions of celestial events, the author invites his readers to seek out the literal, allegorical, and moral dimensions of his fantastic, dream-like scenes, and beyond these to reach to the ultimate spiritual or mystical sense. As midrash, the work would consist of pervasive allusions to Old Testament statements from beginning to end.

> If we wonder what the average Christian in the churches of Asia could make of this, we should remember that the strongly Jewish (sic!) character of most of these churches made the Old Testament much more familiar than it is even to well-educated modern Christians. But we should also remember the circle of Christian prophets in the churches (cf. 22:9, 16) who would probably have studied, interpreted and expounded John's prophecy with the same kind of learned attention they gave to the Old Testament prophecies (Bauckham 1993: 18).

Nearly all commentators agree that the book of Revelation really is without peer among the documents of antiquity. There are similar accounts of visions (the books of Enoch, Daniel, 4 Ezra),

but all these were not written by the persons who claim to have
written them; they are called "pseudepigraphal." There are also
midrashic documents, but nothing like a whole document that simply weaves a tissue of allusions to the Old Testament without cit-
ing the passages to which the author alludes. Despite these major
category difficulties, interpreters remain undaunted and continue
to explain what the book has to say (see Bauckham 1993: 1–22).

1. Ancient Astronomy as the Type of Writing of Revelation

Nearly a century ago and subsequently, a number of scholarly
historians have called attention to the fact that the type of writing,
imagery, and vocabulary of John's visions in the book of Revelation are typical of ancient astronomy and astrology. The two were
not distinguished in antiquity. Scholars such as Franz Cumont
(1898; 1912; 1919), Franz Boll (1903; 1914), Wilhelm Gundel
(1936a; 1936b; 1950), and André Festugière (1950) were quite
correct in suggesting that the astronomic report is the closest contemporary genre of this book (see Malina 1995). What these studies indicate is that John the seer can and must be taken at his
word. If he says that he went into the sky and looked around, he
obviously believed that he was in the sky and looked around. He
was neither fabricating fiction nor composing midrash. What he
saw is what he said he saw, not an allegory for something else.

Unfortunately, nearly all popular commentators look for theological relevance for today's Christians as they offer allegorical
explanations (see Chevalier 1996: 126–174 for an overview).
Some of these presumably are "historical," showing John's message to his oppressed and anxious churches, persecuted by Rome,
alias Babylon. Others are "prophetic," demonstrating how John's
words look precisely to the twenty-first century, with veiled but
totally obvious reference to Russia, Washington, the oil-rich
Middle East, and even to modern Israel, a U.N.-founded entity
populated largely by ethnic Khazars (also known as Ashkenazi
Jews), the descendants of ninth-century A.D. Jewish converts from
Central Russia!

Finally, a further group of scholarly commentators on Revelation spend endless pages making sure the author's presumed Torah allusions are clearly spelled out, thus making the book of Revelation "little more than a midrash of the Old Testament via the Apocrypha and Pseudepigrapha" (Moore 1982: 91), composed by an academic with the traditions of Israel solely on his mind (e.g., see Flusser 1988: 390–485). In fact, there are frequent allusions to Israel's sacred writings, but to focus on them is to miss the proverbial forest for the trees. The forest here is the celestial skyscape.

The Revelation of John consists of descriptions of the author's visions of events in the sky. The final but secondary framework of this work is that of a Hellenistic letter directed to John's fellow Jesus-group prophets (Rev 1:9; 19:10; 22:9). In other words, the work was not being sent to "the average Christian in the churches of Asia" (Bauckham 1993: 18), as most commentators believe. It is quite significant to be cognizant of the fact that the democratization of the New Testament writings took place only with the Reformation! In antiquity, writings containing revelation from God (or the gods) were not meant for just anybody, not even for just any "Christian." The visions of John are for his fellow Jesus-group prophets, who would, presumably, impart their meaning to their Jesus-groups with proper explanation.

For members of these Jesus-groups, the focal question was neither the delay of Jesus' coming as Israel's Messiah (the so-called Parousia) nor some catastrophic end of the world. Rather, as present-oriented, first-century Mediterraneans in a ruralized, peasant society, their concerns were with the here and now (Malina 1996b): What is the Lord Jesus doing now for us? What does Jesus' present activity have to do with the recent destruction of Jerusalem? What are we to gain by continued faith in the God who raised Jesus from the dead? In Israelite tradition, persons who provided answers to such questions were prophets of various types. The visionary John of Patmos, along with the addressees of his visions, belonged to the ranks of such prophets.

In this document John intimates that he was a member of the house of Israel who had joined the Israelite messianic group that perceived the resurrected Jesus as God's exalted one (Rev 1:9). He was "in spirit," that is, in an altered state of consciousness (see Pilch 1993; 1995; 1996; references are in Rev 1:10; 4:2; 17:3; 21:10; it is identical to "the hand of the Lord" in 1 Kgs 18:46; Ezra 7:6, 28; Ezek 1:3; 3:14, 22; 8:1, 3; 33:22; 37:1; 40:1; Acts 11:21; 13:11; for further information, see Malina and Pilch 2000). In his altered state of consciousness, he finds answers in the sky to the questions of where Jesus is now, what Jesus is doing now, and what that means for us in our present situation. It seems that John's fellow group members knew of the destruction of Jerusalem. They experienced temptations to disloyalty and hoped for life with God and his Messiah, now cosmic Lord, Jesus. The book of Revelation is a description of this prophet's sky journeys and experiences described in terms of Israel's normative intertext, the Torah, and by a person who believes that God has raised Jesus from the dead.

The author and his fellow prophets lived at the end of the first century A.D. Therefore they shared no Enlightenment or Romantic values. They had no sense of history, not even "salvation history," and they did not work with the nineteenth-century categories of "fact" and "fiction." They were little concerned with individualistic values; they were not aware of universal values. Rather, they were non-introspective, collectivistically oriented persons with no idea of our contemporary notions of psychology (Prickett 1996; Malina 1996c). Socially, they were persons living at the overlap of Mediterranean and Middle Eastern cultural spheres in the ancient advanced agricultural peasant societies of their times. As collectivistic persons, they defined themselves in terms of the groups to which they belonged. Since they were non-introspective and not psychologically minded, they believed that what happened to them happened because someone else, some person external to themselves, was in control (Malina and Neyrey 1991; 1996). The big question was whether they were or were not responsible for what occurred in their lives, not whether they could change their world. Since they were not in control of their lives or anything else that befell them, John the seer revealed who in fact was in control and how this control was exercised. They did not need to be alarmed by conflicting claims of those who offered competing views: political, political-religious, philosophical, etc. (Malina 1992; 1995).

John's revelation comes in his altered state of consciousness experience that propels him into the sky. In this state he confronts a range of sky beings: angels, holy ones, comets and stars, and enthroned above all, a single God (for details, see Malina 1995). He describes what he sees in terms of Israelite tradition expressed by such astral prophets as Ezekiel, Zechariah, Daniel, Enoch, and Jesus himself (Malina 1997). It was rather common knowledge at the time that stars, either singly or in constellations, were living, personal beings, generally more powerful than God's sky servants or angels or the holy ones in God's entourage or the sky winds or spirits before the celestial throne.

> Aside from the Epicureans, all the major philosophical schools in the Hellenistic era believed in the divinity of the stars. Even the notorious atheist Euhemerus (fl. 300 B.C.) acknowledged that they (at least) were gods. . . . If one supposes, as later Platonism usually did, that stars were composed of soul and body, of sensible and intelligible, of superior and inferior, of ruling and ruled, one would think that only the soul of the star would be divine, and not its body. One response was to say that in the case of the stars, soul was perfectly adapted to body, and the lower and visible part to a higher intelligible part. The "secondary" gods exist through the higher invisible gods, depending on them as the star's radiance depends on the star. In the star the divine soul exercises a perfect supremacy (Scott 1991: 55 and 57).

From the point of view of the first-century Mediterranean perception of the sky, the whole cast of characters in the book of Revelation consisted of celestial phenomena: constellations, stars, planets, and comets that shared the sky below the supreme God and his celestial entourage: angels, holy ones, spirits, etc. Each celestial object in the book was a celestial entity, whether full of eyes or not ("eyes" in the sky was a synonym for stars). As was usual at the time, comets were called bowls, trumpets, horses, and the like, and comets always portended negative effects. My concern here is not to describe the sky as seen by the author throughout the book but rather to focus on the meaning of the vision of the city in the sky now descending from God and the wedding of this city with the cosmic Lamb (see Malina 1993a; 1995).

In sum, the type of writing pattern or genre of Revelation is that of a first-century Mediterranean astronomical/astrological document describing the celestial visions of an Israelite astral prophet who believed in the resurrected Lord Jesus. His reading of the sky and its living entities provided him with a message for his fellow believers. The burden of his message is "do not be deceived" (see Pilch 1994). The reason for this message is that he, in fact, knew what was going on, thanks to the celestial visions, which he shared with his fellow prophets, to be mediated to their respective churches.

2. Overview of the Book of Revelation

John of Patmos begins his account by telling his audience how he was "in spirit" and came to see Jesus as a celestial phenomenon, as cosmic *Polokrator,* cosmic Lord in control of the sky. This cosmic Lord commands John to deliver seven edicts to the angels (or sky servants) of seven churches in Asia Minor.

After this opening vision covering chapters 1–3, the first section of the work describes John taking to the sky and beholding God enthroned above the vault of the sky, surrounded by twenty-four elders, with four animate beings at each corner of this throne room (4:4, 6). A Lamb, situated as though slain, appears and is pronounced worthy to open the scroll of God's decree. As the Lamb proceeds to open the scroll, each living creature takes a turn at summoning God's angels to let loose some celestial event. And each celestial event produces gradually increasing destruction on the land of Israel, concluding at the "city in which they crucified their Lord" (11:8). The whole scenario, replete with cosmic music, comes to a close with God's sky temple visible to the seer at the close of chapter 11 (11:19).

A second section of the work runs from chapters 12 to 16, where we are introduced to a pregnant woman in the sky, giving birth to a son, who is swooped up "to God and to his throne" (12:5), while a celestial dragon lies in wait to devour the child. This dragon is soon joined by two other creatures—a sea beast and a land beast—and they, too, wreak havoc on the newly created land.

The third section, chapters 17–19, is viewed from a cosmic mountain and depicts a devastated Babylon, the first city built after the biblical flood (see Gen 11:4). The fate of this city is sealed by a final battle in the sky, which is followed by the fourth and final vision. The final vision consists in the emergence from the sky of the celestial Jerusalem (chaps. 20–21), descending like a bride for her wedding to the cosmic Lamb, whom we encountered at the beginning of the book of visions. (Figure 1 below, translated and adapted by Malina [1995: 166] from Milik [1976], presents a reconstructed map of the world with celestial mountains, seas, and wilderness duly in place. This map underlies the descriptions of 1 Enoch 1–36; it was first developed by Grelot [1958], who claimed that its parentage derived from the *Enuma Elish,* the Babylonian account of creation, and Homer; Milik [1976: 40] further adapted it and claimed that the author of the book of Revelation held the same view of the world.)

What are we to make of all these sights? As noted above, most modern commentators think that we have some sort of apocalyptic eschatology, a description of the end of the world. Others treat the work as an extended allegory, of the sort indicated by the two rather brief allegorical passages in the work itself (the exalted *Polokrator* in 1:20 and the sky servant in 17:8-18). These allegories derive, we are told, either from midrashic methods common in Israel or from allusion to sky phenomena standing for ongoing political realities. Most modern commentators believe that the work is a literary fiction, a symbolic allegorical narrative composed by an author with an active literary imagination envisioning the transformation of some dimension of life (again, see the brief history in Chevalier 1997: 126–174).

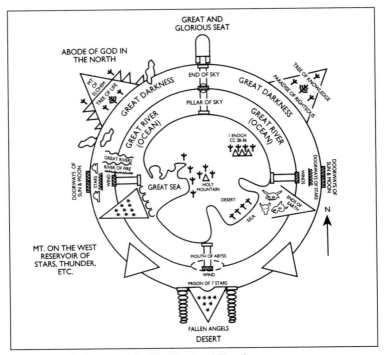

Figure 1: John's Map of the World, after 1 Enoch

On the other hand, various "heretical" groups singled out by Hippolytus (d. 235) in his *Refutation of All Heresies* interpreted the sky in much the same way as the author of Revelation did. They, too, saw biblical personages in the configuration of the stars: Adam, Eve, the serpent, and the like. For example, Hippolytus reports how some (ostensibly of the Israelite tradition) interpreted the sky both with the Bible and in order to understand the Bible. These interpreters began with the scholarship of the period provided by Aratus in a famous astronomical poem called *The Phenomena:*

> Aratus says that there are in the sky revolving, that is, gyrating stars, because from east to west, and west to east, they journey perpetually, (and) in an orbicular figure. And he says (V, 45–46) that there revolves towards "the Bears" themselves, like some stream of a river, an enormous and prodigious monster, (the)

Serpent; and that this is what the devil says in the book of Job to the Deity, when (Satan) uses these words: "I have traversed earth under heaven, and have gone around (it)" (Job 1:7), that is, that I have been turned around and thereby have been able to survey the worlds. For they suppose that towards the North Pole is situated the Dragon, the Serpent, from the highest pole looking upon all (the objects), and gazing on all the works of creation, in order that nothing of the things that are being made may escape his notice. For though all the stars in the firmament set, the pole of this (luminary) alone never sets, but careening high above the horizon, surveys and beholds all things, and none of the works of creation, he says, can escape his notice (*Refutation of All Heresies,* IV, xlvii, ed. A. Roberts and J. Donaldson, in ANF 5, 42–43).

We consider the book of Revelation the result of John's astronomical observation and interpretation of a sequence of sky visions. After an introductory vision that forms part of John's letter, the work proceeds with four major scenes. The first tells of his experiences of the sky scenarios that result in the fate of Judea and its central place, Jerusalem (chaps. 4–11). His second scene describes the antediluvian situation of creation (chaps. 12–16). The third scene looks to the fate of the first postdiluvian city of humankind, Babel/Babylon (chaps. 17–20). And the fourth scene is the vision of the celestial Jerusalem to be wedded to the Lamb in the presence of God (chaps. 21–22).

In the following chapter we will provide scenarios for reading about the holy city, the new Jerusalem, that descends from God in the sky. What sort of a city was the new Jerusalem? Was it a Rome or Athens in the sky? What sorts of cities are to be found in the sky? In fact, what is a city? After presenting a set of scenarios and outfitting those scenarios with some first-century appurtenances, we consider the new Jerusalem as bride. What was the significance of the references to the wedding of the cosmic Lamb and the new Jerusalem noted by the prophet John in the book of Revelation? How does a cosmic Lamb marry a celestial city? John obviously thought he was making sense to his audience, since his work is a "revelation," not a concealment.

Interpretation explains what is taken for granted and unmentioned in a document. Some societies value low-context communications; they expect people to spell out as much as they can when they write something as learned as a description of an encounter with God. Other societies value high-context verbal interactions; people are presumed to know nearly everything the other person really has to say. High-context authors assume that their audience understands nearly everything they leave unsaid in their compositions. The non-philosophical writings of antiquity were notably high-context documents. This, of course, includes John's descriptions of his visions in the book of Revelation.

Our interpretation begins by supplying information about the nature of a city in antiquity, followed by an explanation of the description of the Jerusalem located in the sky, as perceived by first-century Mediterraneans in the Jesus tradition. It concludes with an explanation of the description of the cosmic Lamb and of that Lamb's wedding with the celestial city. Since all this takes place in the sky, and since it is reported in a first-century Mediterranean document, it is not a misplaced emphasis to employ ancient astronomy/astrology as key to the author's context.

3

The Holy City in the Sky

We now turn to the final vision of the book of Revelation. The astral prophet John sets forth his theological presuppositions throughout his work. From what he has previously written in the earlier chapters, we know that he sees God's will laid out in the sky. He reads celestial phenomena through the lenses of Israel's scriptures and his experience in his Jesus-movement group. For our author, what the new sky and the new land hold in store for his readers is life with God. And this entails the Lamb of God wedded to a celestial city—the cosmic Jesus wedded to a new Jerusalem.

A fuller analysis of the seer's theological insights requires a culturally sensitive inquiry into the nature of the sky city in the author's estimation. To facilitate our understanding of his theological insights, I should like to ask: What was a city for the author and his audience? What does such a city of God mean? What were its ramifications, structures, and values, and how do these fit into Israel's traditions?

If we seek to understand the meaning of the celestial city, the new Jerusalem, we have to look into the relevant dimensions of the prevailing first-century social systems. The first question is, Whose specific social system shall we use? As previously noted, ancient Mediterranean writings are, as a rule, high-context documents (see Malina 1996a). Authors assume that their audience will understand far more than is expressed in their compositions. Our problem is to supply what a first-century audience could readily supply.

The author of Revelation labels the celestial city as a "holy city" and "new Jerusalem." He describes it in terms of its concrete architectural configurations, and he interprets some of these configurations for us by telling us that there are city walls, pierced by gates at regular intervals. The walls are built of precious stones. Inside the walls is a city square of sorts, a forum, while water is abundant, and life-sustaining vegetation is readily available. Quite notably, the city lacks a temple. Instead, God himself, with the cosmic Lamb, is enthroned at the center of the city.

With these minimal data we are supposed to have enough information to understand what this city means, what is the action or goal that this configuration is meant to realize in its quest for collective action. One reason for this is that Israel's tradition was quite cognizant of a celestial Jerusalem (see the study of Söllner [1998], which reviews this tradition in 1 Enoch 14 and 24–27; Tobit 13 and 14; Sirach 36 and 51; Baruch 5; Psalms of Solomon 11; Qumran Psalms; Sibylline Oracles 3; Qumran Scrolls 4Q554, 5Q15; Gal 4:21-31; Heb 11–13; and 4 Ezra 7–10). Yet John's description is distinctive in several ways, as we shall note.

1. First-Century Mediterranean "Cities"

From the information about first-century Mediterranean social systems that we now possess, it is quite clear that the so-called first urban Christians were nothing of the sort imaginable by persons at the beginning of the twenty-first century. Nothing in today's "urban" experience comes close to what the ancients referred to as city life. First of all, with broad local variation, daily life in that period was daily life in the Roman Empire. Secondly, given the past two thousand years of development in the West, society in the Mediterranean region of the period is best characterized as a ruralized society (Southall [1998] also uses this designation).

What I mean by ruralized society is that great landowners set the agenda for the empire on the basis of their interests, values, and concerns. This point should be clearer from the following considerations. It is a truism among urban historians that the U.S. at present is an *urbanized* society (Hays 1993). Urban areas contain most of the national population, and urban agendas determine national policies (see Ebner et al. 1993). Urban concerns dominate the goals, values, and behaviors of the five percent of the population that is engaged in agricultural production.

Our urbanized society is quickly developing into one with a global outreach. Before it became urbanized, the U.S. became an *urban* society over the period marked by the rise of industrialization to the end of the Second World War. An urban society, in this perspective, is one in which a significant proportion of the population lives and works in urban centers, following an agenda quite different from that of rural society yet in somewhat tandem rhythms. In urban societies, urban agendas compete with rural ones in determining national policies. Urban and rural agendas foster conflicting goals, values, and behaviors. Before the waves of immigration at the end of the nineteenth century and the first quarter of the twentieth, the U.S. was essentially a *rural* society, with rural agendas determining national policies and rural concerns dominating the goals, values, and behaviors of the 95 percent of the population living on the land and the 5 percent living permanently in cities.

A careful perusal of the following comparative chart will underscore the differences between ancient central places embedded in ruralized societies and modern cities situated in urban industrial and urbanized societies (chart taken from Malina 2000b):

Figure 2: Types of Society

TYPE OF SOCIETY			
Ruralized Society	**Rural Society II: Urban Depot Society**	**Urban Industrial Society**	**Urbanized Society**
Ancient *polis/civitas*	Medieval city City before the Industrial Revolution	Industrial Revolution city	Agglomerative urban areas

CITY TYPE			
Administrative central places	Depot cities	Industrial cities	Informational cities
CITY FOCUS			
Central place is a bundle of consumption demands and pressures locally satisfied from subsistence by force.	Central place is a bundle of consumption demands and pressures satisfied from surplus by reciprocity.	Central place is a bundle of consumption demands and pressures stimulated by technology needs.	Central place is a bundle of consumption demands and pressures stimulated by marketing agents
Necessities	Necessities City conveniences	Necessities City conveniences Personal conveniences	Necessities City conveniences Personal conveniences Amenities
Food, clothing, shelter	Food, clothing, shelter City technology	Food, clothing, shelter City technology Personal technology	Food, clothing, shelter City technology Personal technology Information
ROADS			
Roads: local patterns to central place	Roads: Intercity patterns	Roads: Industrial interregional patterns	Roads: Global patterns
SOURCE OF TECHNOLOGY			
Technology of rural origin	Technology of rural origin	Technology of city origin: Mechanic	Technology of city origin: Electronic
MEANING OF OPEN PLACES			
Open places: wilderness and desert, to be avoided	Open places: wilderness and desert, to be avoided	Open places out there for industrial waste disposal	Open places out there—lands, rivers, air, oceans and ground water—off limits to waste disposal.

CITIZENS

Citizens are large landholding city elites or those of value to city elites	Citizens are city residents	Citizens are nationals Type I	Citizens are nationals Type II

ELITES

Elites are agriculturalists	Elites are merchants	Elites are urban industrialists and bankers	Elites are urban information managers

LABOR FORCE

Agricultural labor force	Mercantile labor force	Industrial labor force	Informational labor force

SCOPE OF COMMUNICATION

Local communication	Interurban communication	Regional communication	Global communication

EMPIRE CONTROL

Elite agriculturalists control empire	Elite merchants control empire	Elite urbanites control national empire	Elite urbanites control multinational empire

SURPLUS CONTROL

Agricultural "surplus" wrested and controlled by force	Agricultural surplus controlled by pact	Agricultural surplus controlled by monopoly	Agricultural surplus controlled by market

AGRICULTURE CONTROL

Owner/producers control agricultural products	Warehousers control agricultural products	Processors control agricultural products	Marketers control agricultural products
Crops determined by owner/growers = staples	Crops determined by growers and elite demands = staples	Crops determined by processors and market demands	Crops determined by marketers and created market demands

AGRICULTURE CONTROL (cont.)

Inalienable land now considered alienable; all land taken – region without central place was "desert"	Alienable land Feudal and communal ownership	Alienable land Abandoned land becomes public land	Alienable land Private and public ownership

RESIDENCE

Elites have country estates and city houses	Elites live in city or in country houses	Elites have city/country houses	Non-elites have city/country houses

NATURE

Natural world is source of commodities; extractive farm and forest elite economy; wild nature to be destroyed and controlled	Natural world is source of commodities; extractive farm and forest elite economy; wild nature to be destroyed and controlled	Natural world is source of commodities; extractive farm and forest industrialists but wild nature to be controlled and preserved for industrial work force	Natural world is to be maintained in a pristine state for its own sake. This is nature urbanized: preservation of wilderness, wild animals, wetlands, rivers, biodiversity, old growth, or natural areas
Rivers are uncontrollable	Rivers are uncontrollable; to be used for transport	Rivers are to be tamed for industrial use	Rivers are to be left in or returned to natural state, "wild and scenic rivers"
Wilderness, like desert, is to be feared	Wilderness to be avoided	Wilderness to be tamed for industrial use	Wilderness to be appreciated and enjoyed
Consumptive view of wildlife	Consumptive view of wildlife	Consumptive view of wildlife as industrial value	Appreciative view of wildlife: to be enjoyed, studied, observed

CITY RESIDENTS			
City people were rural people, living within their collective resources. Subsistence society	City people no longer rural people, living off new abundance	City people were never rural people, living off new national superabundance	City people are never rural people, now living off national and global resources

The fact is that first-century Mediterraneans lived in ruralized societies, not in urbanized societies (see Ramage 1983; Sanjek 1990; Hays 1993). This, of course, includes those living in "cities." And even in cities, the problems people faced were not what we call "urban" problems. The fact that these people dwelt in central places called *poleis* or *civitates* (Greek and Latin, respectively, for "cities") did not make them "urbanites," as we might experience the phenomenon. Socially speaking, ruralized societies did not have middle classes, minorities, nuclear families, future orientations, market-based economies, or any other categories by which we assess our contemporary urbanized societies (see Rohrbaugh 1991a; 1991b; 1996). Technologically, ruralized societies were limited to energy provided by animals, humans, and rudimentary fireboxes (outdoor ovens, braziers, no chimneys).

In these societies the great landowners, who shaped the agenda of daily life for society at large, were considered the "best" people. These "aristocrats" generally had two places of residence: a city residence and a country estate. The city residence was a house built as part of a cluster of such houses of other landowning elites in a central or nodal place, the city (see Rohrbaugh 1991; Oakman 1991). Just as small holders lived in houses clustered together, usually for support and protection, in towns and villages, so too did the large holders cluster together; but their housing clusters formed the center of what the ancients called a *polis* or *civitas*.

The first-century Mediterranean city was really a large, ruralized central place in which properly pedigreed "farmers/ranchers" displayed and employed their unbelievable wealth in competitions for honor among one another. Large holders thus found it in their interest to live periodically near other large holders in central places that likewise provided them with organized force (an army) to protect their interests from the vast masses of other persons. The elite united to promote and defend their collective honor in face of the outgroup in annual rites of war, which, if carried off successfully, brought them more land and/or the produce of that land. They equally participated in the continual, if seasonal, activity of extortion called taxation. Their honor rating rooted in kinship brought them the power that brought them further wealth.

However, for these elites, the city house was a secondary dwelling. It was not a private place like the dwellings of the city non-elites. Rather, the elite city house was multifunctional, a place of constant socializing, economic and sometimes political intercourse, and not simply a place of habitation. For these elites, living together essentially served the purpose of daily challenge-riposte interaction in the pursuit of honor.

The primary elite residence was the country estate, a place of residence and subsistence (family plus land and buildings for production, distribution, transmission, reproduction, group identification). Non-elite farmers and tenants imagined their limited holdings in terms of the ideal—the elite country estate. Elite country houses were spacious, centrally heated, with a swimming bath, library, works of art, etc. They were situated on vast agricultural estates worked by slaves in the West and largely by tenants in the East.

Carney notes that "the gulf between an ancient city and a modern one is immense" (Carney 1975: 86; see Weaver and White 1972; White and Weaver 1972; Oakman 1991). The gulf is so great because the development of the "complexified crowd container" that we call a city has gone through several step-level changes, as indicated in Figure 2. Consider the differences between spiders, sparrows, squid, and squirrels, or between bees, bobolinks, bullheads, and bears. All these creatures are animals. But how many people consider life in a beehive or in a spider web typical of animal life? Having a spider in one's kitchen is not the same as having a lion in one's living room. And yet, to say that one has an animal in the house, referring to the spider, is as misleading as talking about the "first urban Christians," as though they had anything "urban" in common with us today.

With Figure 2 in hand, we might attempt an intellectual experiment and move from the modern city to the city forms of antiquity. The first thing to note is that such a move requires that we pass through a whole series of intermediary forms, each resting on some preceding form that is less complexified than what followed. What characterizes modern Western civilization is information technology rooted in industrialization. The contemporary city form is the megalopolis. What enabled this city form to develop was triggered by the public health revolution, in which for the first time population increase came from city-born babies. Actually it was not too long ago that the healthier countryside had poured its population into what had been an urban deathtrap. It took the industrial revolution and innovative transportation technology to bring about the conurbations that we think of as major cities. Nation-states, the invention of the nineteenth century, normally have several major cities. More than 40 percent of the gross national product of such nation-states and their cities is spent on information, while 5 percent of the population grows enough food to feed the rest and many others besides.

Modern cities are more fully developed forms of the many smokestack cities that emerged during the period of industrialization in the nineteenth century. While industrial cities, with their slums and confined quarters, are a sorry contrast in some regards to farm-town living, they do represent a new type of city in comparison with the medieval town. Medieval towns were largely market centers that emerged as a result of the agricultural revolution of the Middle Ages and the new, deep-furrowing plow (see Randsborg 1989; Delong and Shleifer 1993). People moved into rather dingy, ill-smelling, unlit, and poorly heated clustered housing to deal with the agricultural surplus that was stored and traded in the medieval city. Agricultural surplus was enough to allow for the support and construction of cathedrals, medieval schools, rather elegant town halls and residences for the elites. Medieval societies spent some 40 percent of their gross national product on the new technologies of milling, new plows, warfare, building construction, and shipping. Ninety-five percent of the population was engaged in agriculture, and 5 percent of the population lived in towns, enjoying the agricultural surplus in significant ways.

In many respects, the medieval cities marked significant regression from their predecessors in terms of hygiene, public facilities, and visual appeal. Yet the agricultural revolution did allow for a new beginning after the general demise of the ancient Mediterranean cities. The great cities of Byzantium and early Rome were based on the aristocratic control of extremely few elites, who could extort wealth from imperial subjects by means of force. Byzantium introduced street lighting, hospitals, and orphanages to the Roman contributions of sewers, aqueducts, amphitheaters, central heating, baths, and parks. Greeks introduced the forum/marketplace, public buildings for legislative councils, theaters, gymnasia, and libraries. Finally, ancient Mesopotamian cities were characterized by temples, palaces, and warehouse-caravansary type buildings (storage complexes). As in the Middle Ages, most of the population was tied to agriculture and the land. The "gross imperial product" was devoted, for the most part, to food, clothing, and shelter, along with showpiece construction in the cities that glorified the elite patrons who paid for them (through surplus from landholdings).

While there were no nations or nation-states in antiquity, every civilized "people" had one "mother city" (called a *metropolis* in Greek). The mother city was typically a very large primate city, beside which all the community's other cities and towns were insignificant. Rome, for instance, and later Constantinople each had the population of an entire province within and around their walls. Philo, a Hellenistic philosopher living in Alexandria, called Jerusalem "a metropolis" for the several million persons of the house of Israel who had immigrant enclaves all over the Eastern Mediterranean (*Flaccus* 7, 46; *Leg.* 36, 281; see Runia 1989; for a list of these emigrants, see Acts 2:9-11, where they are described as "Judeans, devout men from every nation under the sky"). Moreover, each metropolis, in its day, was where the action was—political, social, and intellectual. The primate city of antiquity was the nerve center of an ethnic region and/or of an empire (Carney 1975: 85–86).

More specifically, Duncan Jones provides a further contrast between the modern and the Greco-Roman city:

> In modern usage city population usually means those who live within a built-up area called a city, and perhaps includes those living in a narrow adjoining periphery. The typical situation in the Roman world was radically different. Most of the countryside as a whole belonged to the territory of one city or another. City territories were thus of substantial size, and their native inhabitants normally counted among the inhabitants of each city. Juridically, though not always in practice, they were as much local citizens as were the urban residents (Duncan Jones 1984: 252).

The ordinary "secondary" *polis* was not necessarily an important residential center in itself. It was a civilized (that is, Hellenized) nucleus for those who were able to live away from the soil; it also offered its facilities to those living outside the town. It was the main center of worship in a region, and many of its public buildings were temples and shrines, although there were shrines on the country estates of elites. Pliny thought it necessary to rebuild a temple on his estate (on religious advice), for the benefit of the crowd from the whole district that assembled at the shrine on one day each year (*Epist.* 9, 39).

Furthermore, the secondary *polis* was the center of administration, legal decisions, commerce, hygiene and medicine, social life, and entertainments. To some extent the proliferation of *polis* monuments was the result of the Roman affinity for the grandiose rather than the fulfillment of genuine social needs. Nevertheless, the abundance of large public buildings in a Roman *polis* and the high proportion of the built-up area that they often occupied also suggest that the *polis* unit existed for the use of a community larger than could be contained in the houses within the built-up area. Similarly, the wealth needed to construct these buildings was typically drawn from sources extending well beyond the *polis* walls.

Duncan Jones offers some population figures for ancient cities (as distinct from units such as tribes) under the late republic and empire. Alexandria in Egypt had more than 300,000 free inhabitants at the end of the republic (Diodorus 17.2.6). Carthage came to rival Alexandria, perhaps exceeding it in size in the early third century (Herodian 7.6.1); apparently Carthage had more than overtaken Alexandria by the fourth century (Ausonius *Ord urb nob*. 2 and 5). Antioch in

Syria was nearly equal to Alexandria under Augustus and was still its rival in the fourth century (Strabo 16.2.5; Ausonius *Ord urb nob.* 4). Pergamum in the second century A.D. had a free adult population of about 80,000, and about 40,000 slaves, implying a total population of about 180,000, including children (Galen 5, 49). Ephesus had at least 40,000 male citizens, and thus a population probably no smaller than that of Pergamum, from the terms of a gift made in the second or early third century A.D. ff. Apamea in Syria had 117,000 free inhabitants in a census taken under Augustus (*ILS* 2683). The civitas Aeduorum in Gaul was assessed as having 32,000 *libera capita* under Constantine, probably adult citizens of both sexes, and thus a free population of 50,000 to 55,000 (*Panegyricus* VIII.2). Centuripae in Sicily had 10,000 male citizens, and thus perhaps 35,000 free inhabitants about 70 B.C. (Cicero *Verr.* 2.2.163). (Cited in paraphrase from Duncan Jones 1984: 253.)

What was life like in an ancient Mediterranean metropolis? Carney offers the following description:

> Our image of a city of antiquity, however, would be very different according to our status. If we were a member of the Roman elite, for instance, we would leave our country house— spacious, centrally heated, with a swimming bath, library, works of art, etc.—and estate, and drive, ride or be carried in a litter to the city. We would pass the tombs of the great along the highway nearer to the city. Our entourage would make a way for us through the teeming city streets. We would thus make our way through the city centre, past splendid theatres, amphitheatres, public halls and baths and parks. Eventually we would be welcomed by yet more attendants in our town house, which would be almost as elegant as our country house—and largely supplied with foodstuffs by our country estate. There our clients would be waiting to dance attendance upon us.
>
> If we were poor, however, our day in Rome would start in a noisome tenement. There would be no central heating; possibly a charcoal brazier (chimneys had not yet been invented). There would be no running water, no toilet (slops were tossed from the window—for which glass panes had yet to be invented). An oil lamp would light our room, sparsely furnished for want of money and for fear of wall-breakers (as burglars were known). We would

don our dirty, louse-ridden outer clothing and plunge down as many as six flights of stairs into the teeming mass of humanity outside. A meal from a street vendor whose stall obstructed the press of human traffic in the street might follow, if we had time and money a wheaten cake or some fruit, maybe. Then a drink from a fountain—tea, coffee and chocolate were as yet unknown. Then to our day's work. This might be labor in a brick-works, or running errands for some dignitary or other or some such, if we were fortunate enough to have a job currently. Or it might merely be visiting the homes of those of the great by whose arrogant slave flunkeys we would be grudgingly recognized.

We would accordingly push through the throng, probably with running nose or hacking cough if it were winter, or feeling slightly aguish if it were summer. The noisome twisting streets between the tall tenements of the slums would give way to broader streets flanked by the windowless exteriors of the one-storey houses of the wealthy or the shop fronts of the two-storey houses of the moderately well-to-do. We might catch a preoccupied glimpse of some of "their" big, important public buildings, or even jostle our way along a portico or two. But we probably would not move out of "our" quarter of the city—"our" section of the slums plus their adjacent good residential area and well-appointed public places. A man had to be careful in this violent city world of tough soldiers, sneaky cutpurses and other desperate, poor men (Carney 1975: 85–86).

From all that has been said, it is clear that we know much about the ancient Mediterranean city. And the developmental line for European cities running from Greece, Rome, Byzantium, the Middle Ages, early industrialization, and modern megalopolis seems quite fixed. Are any of these city scenarios useful for imagining Jerusalem, whether earthly or celestial? Or do we have to reach back to the Mesopotamian city, characterized by temple, palace, and storage buildings?

2. Institutional Dimensions of Cities

There is an institutional dimension of cities to consider if we wish to grasp the immense changes between cities of antiquity and those of today. What were the ancient cities about? For purposes of analysis, social systems consist of institutions, culture/values, and person-types. The larger, fixed phases of social life are called institutions. In our society, social scientists generally distinguish four major institutions: kinship, politics, economics, religion. Of course, there are many subsets of each of these.

Culture is about symbolizing persons, things, and events by endowing them with meaning and feeling. Values are the qualities and directions of behavior taken by symbolized persons, things, and events. Values inhere in value objects. Value objects are those entities that people in a society generally single out as worthy of attention and assessment. The value objects that embody the major qualities and directions of behavior include the self, others, nature, time, space, and the All. Finally, every social system consists of persons who are inculturated to assess themselves and behavior along a scale running from collectivistic (strong group) to individualistic (weak group). Collectivistic persons give primacy to family and group integrity; individualistic persons give primacy to self-reliance.

Social systems, then, consist of persons sharing formulated conceptions of institutions and value objects. Kinship formulates conceptions concerning the naturing and nurturing of human beings. Politics formulates conceptions concerning effective collective action; economics formulates conceptions concerning provisioning society; and religion formulates conceptions of the general order of existence.

In antiquity there were only two explicit and formal social institutions: kinship and politics. The reason for this is that the discovery of the separation of "church and state" (i.e., religion and politics), as well as the separation of "bank and state" (i.e., politics and economics), took place in the eighteenth century A.D. and subsequently. In antiquity and in all societies not affected by the Northern European Enlightenment, religion was and is to be found in both of the free-standing social institutions, that is, kinship and politics. There was kinship or domestic religion and there was political religion, but no religion pure and simple (Malina 1986; 1994; for ancient Israel, now see Albertz 1994: 17–21).

Ancient Mediterraneans were aware of domestic religion (ancestral deities) and domestic economy (producers and consumers were the same). They were equally aware of political religion (temple systems and deities of specific peoples) and political economy (goods and services for elites only). But there was no focus on economics or religion. Hence there would be no economic or religious ranking of any significance in itself to persons of the time. Similarly, unless economic or religious benefits could be converted into kinship or political advantage, such benefits would be socially meaningless and unnoticed.

For example, political religion used the roles, values, and goals of politics in the articulation and expression of religion. Religious functionaries were political personages; focus was on the deity(ies) as source of power and might, expected to provide order, well-being, and prosperity for the body politic and its power-wielders (nobles) to the benefit of subjects. In monarchic city-territories of the Middle East, temples were political buildings, temple sacrifices were for the public good; the deity of the temple had a staff similar to the one a monarch had in the palace (major-domo = high priest; officials of various ranks and grades = priests, levites; temple slaves, etc.). Democratic cities altered monarchic temples into democratic ones, owned and run by city councils or noble council members, with sacrifice offered according to the wishes of the sacrificing entity.

On the other hand, domestic religion used the roles, values, and goals of the household in the articulation and expression of religion. Religious functionaries were domestic personages (notably fathers and, inside the household, mothers as well, oldest sons, ancestors). Focus was on the deity(ies) as source of solidarity, commitment, belonging mediated through ancestors, expected to provide well-being, health, and prosperity for the kin group and its patriarchs to the benefit of family members. The house had its altars and sacred rites (focused on the hearth = symbol of life), with father (patriarch) and mother (first in charge at home) officiating. Deities were tribal and/or household ones (e.g., God of Abraham, Isaac, Jacob, etc.) as well as ancestors who saw to the well-being, prosperity, and fertility of the family members. Domestic religion

seeks meaning through belonging: an ultimately meaningful existence derives from belonging, for example, to a chosen, select, holy
people. In well-ordered societies, it is belonging to the proper
ranks in one's well-ordered society (often called hierarchy; see
Flanagan 1989). In societies in some disarray, it is belonging to
a proper kin and/or fictive kin group (see Malina 1986; 1994;
1996a). The ingroup/outgroup pattern marking kinship boundaries
served as a marker between families, as well as between the kin
group's political unit, and the rest of the world.

If we consider the step-level changes in the development of
cities, we find that contemporary cities have economics as their
focal social institution. The main focus both in microcities and
megacities of the industrialized world is on economics and economic polity. Medieval market cities focused on the political
economy, with elites for the most part coming from the ranks of
prominent persons in the political religion of the period. The
cities of Greco-Roman Hellenism were administrative cities equally
focused on the political economy; central personages were landowning elites of proper kinship groups, that is, with proper ances-
try. Finally, the cities of Mesopotamia were temple cities with
political religion as their focal social institution; elites were ranking players in the political economy, controlling lands and storage
facilities for taxes in kind.

3. What Cities Have in Common

What, in fact, do all cities have in common so that we moderns
can label ancient central places as "cities" in face of all the radical
differences? If we prescind from those differences and move up to
a higher level of abstraction that might embrace only similarities,
what is a city? What does a city mean? *A city is a bounded, cen-
tralized set of social relationships concerned with effective collective action and expressed spatially in terms of architecture and
the arrangement of places.* This definition derives from the considerations of a number of social geographers and historians, for
example, Ebner et al. (1993), Nutini (1972), Sanjek (1990), Weaver

and White (1972), White and Weaver (1972). Max Weber's penchant for the Greek *polis* as the ideal city form (Weber 1958) makes much of what he says of little use for a general definition; see the trenchant criticism of Abu-Lughod (1975) and Nippel (1991); see also Finley (1977). General characteristics of all cities include the following:

1. Cities form central nodes within some broader network of social relations. In this sense, cities are central places within some region and cannot be understood without taking the regional network into account (see Rohrbaugh 1991a; 1991b; 1996).

2. Because they are central nodes, cities are centripetal, in the sense that all populations in the region forming a network with some city live with their attention directed to that city. People who live with their face toward a given central place form a general ingroup. In antiquity these people were residents of the city and its attending villages. The outgroup is formed by people whose face looks toward other cities.

3. Since every city is centripetal, a city is a terminal to which all roads from villages and regions in the surround lead. Even other cities are simply part of the surround leading to the ingroup city. What determines whether a city is a final terminal or not is the awareness of persons living in the city. My city/our city is always a terminal; all others lead to it. This is rooted in the human perception of space and human limitation. In antiquity it was social geography that determined me in my group, that formed the focal note of everything around us (see Sack 1986; Malina 1993a). This arrangement helps to underscore the boundary between ingroup and outgroup. Our city is always the center of the ingroup. Everything leads to us, including other cities, and it is essentially because it is our city that it is the terminal.

4. A city is a way of effectively realizing a range of collective activity by means of some specific arrangement of territoriality. In antiquity, territoriality referred to the delimiting of some geographic area in terms of the persons organically related to the area that they define and delimit. In antiquity, people thought of themselves and the place they occupied as organically linked (Malina and Neyrey 1991; 1996). That geographical place was likewise

the place where their ancestors dwelt and were buried, and the land itself was often given to them by a deity.

Through territoriality, elites claimed dominance of their central place and its surround. This is simply one dimension of the effective collective action that is the goal of political institutions. In antiquity, large numbers of people were required to support the elites and their concerns, both in the country and in the city. Resident city support consisted of retainers that constituted the non-elite central place population.

5. Becoming a rightful resident of a city in antiquity was totally unlike modern Western territoriality, in which simple physical residence endows persons and groups with civic rights and obligations. In antiquity it was group membership on other than territorial criteria that determined who belonged in a given city, specifically some social relationship with ruling elite and other residents of the city (see Malina 1993a). The alien or stranger was one who had no social relationship with ruling elites or other city residents (see Greer 1986; Elliott 1990).

6. While cities are institutions that primarily seek some effective collective action for some population, the specific focus or social goals of a given city depend on the general social system in vogue at the time. In antiquity, the institutions we call economics and religion were embedded in kinship and politics (see Malina 1986; 1994). Hence along with their political functions, often symbolized by the palace and wall, ancient cities likewise pursued political religion and political economy.

7. Political religion means that the roles, goals, and values of the polity serve to articulate and express religion. In theocracies, the temple is a replication of the palace, and temple personnel, interactions, and functions follow the pattern of palace personnel, interactions, and functions. If the palace houses a king with a large body of servants, from prime minister to royal slaves running royal farms to feed palace household and army alike, the temple houses a divine monarch with a large body of servants, from primary major-domo (high priest) to temple slaves running temple lands to feed the temple household and staff alike. In other political forms, temples are usually the concern of local elite

families. In no case are temples directly for the benefit of worshipers, just as palaces are not directly for the benefit of loyal subjects (see Van der Toorn 1995; Wiggermann 1995).

The political economy, of course, means that the roles, goals, and values of the polity serve to articulate and express economics. The chief beneficiaries of the economy are central political personages, whether in palace or temple. The system of taxation and tribute look to the well-being of elites.

8. Given the reality of political religion and political economics and the distinctive features of Greco-Roman and Middle Eastern cities, we might draw up a sort of range of emphases in political institutions of antiquity. In Figure 3, with the political institution at the center and economics and religion on either end, we might rank the city as a theocracy (at one extreme) or as a port of trade (at the other extreme). Moving toward the center on the theocracy side, we have the Middle Eastern city ranging from priestly control to kinship; moving toward the center from the economics side, we have the *polis* or *civitas* in varying degrees: democratic, aristocratic, or monarchic.

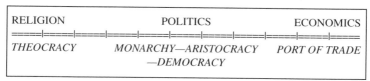

Figure 3: Emphases of Political Institutions in Antiquity

9. The population of cities are stratified (see Flanagan 1989; Malina 2000a). In ancient cities, with their political religions, these stratified populations form hierarchies, with superior personages wielding "sacred power" over lesser personages. Injuries done to superiors is always some form of "sacrilege." This is what hierarchy implies.

Thus to understand the meaning of a city, one must have recourse to the prevailing social system. Whether it is a twenty-first-century Euro-American city or an ancient Mediterranean city, it is from the social system that meaning derives, and it is the meanings of the social system that the city expresses.

Another way to explain this perspective on cities is to compare the meanings mediated by cities with those mediated by language. Just as language encodes meaning from a social system, specifically by means of wordings or patternings, and concretely by means of soundings/spellings, the same is true, *mutatis mutandis,* of a city (see Halliday 1978; for a literary-aesthetic approach, Wiseman 1992). The social-relation dimension of the city, its concern with effective collective action, is the meaning level of a city. All political institutions are concerned with effective collective action. As political institutions, cities of the past have concern for effective collective action as their genus. The specific differences among cities consisted in the historical and cultural features. The spatial articulation of a city in terms of city planning and architecture is the patterning level. The actual materials used to build the city relate to the concrete level of a city. Another way to say this is that the meaning level of the city is social relations, the patterning (wording) level is spatial relation in terms of architecture and place arrangement, and at the concrete (spelling/sounding) level we have stone upon stone. We interpret the stones and other building materials (spelling/sounding) as configured in patterned structures such as walls, palaces, temples, and the like as encoding meanings from the social system. While archaeology puts us in contact with concrete stones, the relationship of stone to stone is part of the wording or patterning level, which in turn encodes or realizes the meaning level, the social relationship level. To understand what a city means, while it is useful to have the documentation that we call an archaeological site or a physical city, in point of fact the meaning expressed by and encoded in streets, buildings, and walls of a city derives from a social system.

From the point of view of what languages express, there are three dimensions to language: the ideational, the interpersonal, and the modal. The ideational refers to what one speaks or writes about; the interpersonal refers to whom one speaks with; and the modal refers to how language realizes the first two aspects. Cities, too, have an ideational, interpersonal, and modal aspect. The ideational aspect points to every feature of a city being about something: streets for travel and meeting, temples for divine residence and audiences, palaces for royal residence and audiences, markets for food and gossip distribution, etc.

The interpersonal aspect points to every feature of a city being about somebody, about persons in statuses and roles. Persons inhabit, utilize, reside, or otherwise occupy the spatial features of a city. In their social relationships city residents wear city architectural features as though they were items of clothing; the buildings and streets tell ahead of time the type of persons to be found in them and the type of activity they would be engaged in.

The modal aspect of language points to every feature of a city being structurally connected and related to other aspects so as to form a complete whole.

Residents in their social relationships form the meaning dimensions of a city. Edifices in a city are the paragraphs and sentences, while the streets in their arrangements form the syntax. Thus every city, with its population, its buildings, and its spatial arrangements, has an ideational, interpersonal, and modal component. Every city says something about its residents and citizens, and it says it to somebody by means of its syntax. Cities are another human way to mean. Cities always mean.

4. The City in the Sky

Now what about our city in the sky? First of all, it is important to note that the presence of a city in the sky, capable of emerging from the sky and descending to the land, was not part of Greco-Roman perceptions. As is well known, scholarly investigation into ancient Greco-Roman cities and their antecedents is rather immense: Anderson (1983), Atherton (1986), Boatwright (1986), Bowman and Rathbone (1992), Boyd and Jameson (1981), Burnell (1992), Burns (1976), Corbier (1991), Eder (1991), Figueira (1991), Finley (1977), Frier (1983), Giovannini (1991), Golding (1975), Gregory (1983), Gruen (1991), Hartigan (1978), Hölscher (1991), Hopkins (1991), Ling (1990), Loraux (1991), Miller (1983), Musiolek (1978), Nutini (1972), Owens (1991), Patterson (1992), Perring (1991), Ramage (1983), Richardson (1991), Scully

(1981; 1990), Stambaugh (1973–74), Thornton (1986), Wallace-Hadrill (1991). Quite useful overviews include those by Cornell (1991), Orr (1983), Raaflaub (1991), Santos Velasco (1994). None of these authors notes anything of a sky-city tradition in the Greek and Roman tradition; rather, it was typical of Middle Eastern lore. Significant studies of Middle Eastern cities include Abu-Lughod (1975), Fisher (1963), Mellaart (1975), Orlin (1975), Wiggermann (1995). Abu-Lughod (1976) demonstrates the continuity of Middle Eastern city traditions in very disparate places. And it was Middle Eastern lore that shaped the temple cities of the Eastern Mediterranean. Consider the following comparative features based on the foregoing studies:

Greco-Roman City	Middle Eastern City
Founder of the city is some hero or heroes.	Founder of the city is some deity.
Originating act is the marking off of the city.	Originating act is the building of a sanctuary/temple.
Political religion is dependent on the devotedness of the elite and their chosen deities.	Political religion is dependent on the deity taking up residence at a given place and those chosen servants of the deity.
Central buildings are primarily for elite political activity, elite residences, and secondarily for the deities.	Central buildings are first and foremost the deity's temple, along with residence for the deity's major-domo(s), and secondly the monarch's palace. Elite residence ranks after these.
Residents are citizens and resident aliens; government is democratic, aristocratic, or tyrannic, i.e., not directly connected with the deity(ies).	Residents are those dedicated to the deity, i.e., servants of the deity, slaves of the deity, with the king as main representative and (son) servant of the deity.
Form of government was consensual, in democratic, timarchic, or monarchic shape.	Form of government was subordinational, essentially a theocracy with a monarch serving as major-domo/servant/son of the central deity.

The purpose of life in the city was the well-being of its citizenry.	The purpose of life in the city was the well-being of the central deity: to know, love, and serve the deity (love = covenantal loyalty).
Taxes and trade exist for the benefit of the city elite.	Taxes and trade exist for the benefit of the central deity and that deity's household, including the monarch. Temple and temple servants including the monarch.
City liturgies are always to the honor of the citizen benefactor.	City liturgies are always to the honor of the deity, redounding upon the deity's special servants.
Citizens and residents are held together by some contractual device, the *societas* or *koinōnia*.	City residents consist of people who are a deity's inheritance, apportioned to the deity "in the beginning" along with territory and sky segment.

The seven Asian cities to whose angels the edicts of Revelation 2–3 were directed were Greco-Roman cities. And there were a goodly number of Greco-Roman cities in Palestine, whether rebuilt or built during the time of Herod the Great and after (for a list, see Sim 1996: 46–47). However, in terms of this comparison, we can say that if there is anything certain about the seer's assessment of his final vision in the book of Revelation, it is that the object of his gaze is not just any sort of city but a Middle Eastern city. The existence of cities in the sky serving as residences for deities has been well known among Mesopotamians for millennia (see especially Wiggermann 1995).

This Mesopotamian perspective is evidenced in Israel as well (e.g., Ezek 48:30-35; Gal 4:26; Sibylline Oracles V, 414–433; 4 Ezra 8:51-52; see Fisher 1963). In this tradition, the earthly temple of the deity was but a pale reflection of the true temple of the deity located in the sky. As a rule this sky temple was located directly above the earthly temple; the earthly city dedicated to the service of the God replicated, in its own way, the spatial arrangements in the sky. Mention of a temple in the sky would presuppose a city in the sky as well, since in the traditional Middle East, cities were adjuncts to temples, serving the needs of the gods residing in the temples (see Malina 1993a).

Of course, John's interpretation of his vision is replete with Israelite allusions. He is, after all, an Israelite prophet in a Jesus-movement group. These allusions begin with his positioning at the remarkable mountain observatory. In order to behold the descending city, the author falls into an altered state of consciousness for another sky journey, this time to a mythically high mountain to bring him as close to the object of his observation as possible (Rev 21:10). This mountain seems to be the very mountain of assembly in the far north beyond the stars and near God's throne (Isa 14:13: "I will set my throne on high; I will sit on the mount of assembly in the far north"). This mountain is the obvious choice as the site for the new Jerusalem, since as Isaiah noted, one day the mountain of the house of the Lord will be the highest of mountains (Isa 2:2; see also Ezek 40:2 and Israelite lore as in 1 Enoch 17:2; see Buxton 1992; Hanson 1994). This is precisely the expectation permeating the author's picture of the new Jerusalem. From his mountain position, the seer studies the descending new city, taking note of its distinctive features (like those in Ezekiel 40–44; see Smith 1986). As an astral prophet of the Resurrected Jesus movement, John reads the traditional Middle Eastern skyscape through Israelite lenses, newly polished and thus refocused by his experience in his Resurrected Jesus-movement group.

5. *The Vision of the Celestial Jerusalem*

What did John see? For those bent on considering John's work as a tissue of midrash, there would have been no real vision. Instead, the work would consist only of a chain of more or less related passages from the Hebrew Bible. In this view, the author was simply "stringing pearls," as latter Jewish authors would say. He simply composed a scenario ultimately derived from allusions to the following well-known intertextual and contemporary resonances in these chapters:

21:1	Isa 65:18; 66:22; 2 Pet 3:13
21:2	Isa 52:1; Rev 3:12; Isa 61:10; Heb 11:10, 16
21:3	Lev 26:11-12; 2 Chr 6:18; Ezek 37:27; Zech 2:10; 2 Cor 6:16
21:4	Isa 25:8; Rev 7:17; Isa 35:10; 65:19
21:5	1 Kgs 22:19; 2 Chr 18:18; Ps 47:8; Isa 6:1; Ezek 1:26-27; Sir 1:8; Rev 4:2, 9; 5:1, 7, 13; 6:16; 7:10, 15; 19:4; 2 Cor 5:17
21:6	Rev 1:8; 22:13; Isa 44:6; 48:12; Rev 1:17; 22:13; Isa 55:1; John 7:37; Rev 22:17; Ps 36:9; Jer 2:13
21:7	2 Sam 7:14
21:8	Isa 30:33; Matt 25:41; Rev 19:20; 20:10, 15; Gen 19:24; Ps 11:6; Ezek 38:22; 3 Macc 2:5; Rev 19:20
21:10	Ezek 40:2
21:11	Isa 60:1, 2, 19
21:12-13	Exod 28:21; Ezek 48:30-35
21:15	Ezek 40:3, 5
21:16-17	Ezek 48:16, 17
21:19	Isa 54:11-12
21:22	Amos 3:13 LXX; 4:13 LXX; Rev 1:8; 4:8; 11:17; 15:3; 16:7, 14; 19:6, 15
21:23	Isa 60:19-20; Rev 22:5
21:24	Isa 60:3, 5; Pss Sol 17:34 (31)
21:25	Isa 60:11; Zech 14:7; Rev 22:5
21:26	Ps 72:10-11; Pss Sol 17:34 (31)
21:27	Isa 52:1; 1 Cor 6:9-10; 2 Pet 3:13; Rev 22:15; Exod 32:32, 33; Ps 69:28; Dan 12:1; Phil 4:3; Rev 3:5; 13:8; 17:8; 20:12, 15
22:1	Ezek 47:1; Joel 3:18; Zech 14:8
22:2	Gen 2:9; 3:22; Ezek 47:12
22:3	Zech 14:11
22:4	Ps 17:15; 42:2; Matt 5:8; Rev 3:12
22:5	Zech 14:7; Rev 21:25; Isa 60:19-20; Rev 21:23; Dan 7:18, 27; Rev 5:10; 20:6
22:6	Dan 2:28, 29, 45; Rev 1:1, 19
22:7	Rev 2:10; 3:11; 22:12, 20
22:8-9	Acts 10:25-26; Rev 19:10

22:10	Dan 12:4; Rev 1:3
22:12	Rev 2:16; 3:11; 22:7, 20; Isa 40:10; 62:11; Ps 28:4; 62:12; Prov 24:12; Isa 59:18; Jer 17:10; Rom 2:6; 1 Cor 3:8; 2 Cor 11:15; 2 Tim 4:14; 1 Pet 1:17; Rev 2:23; 18:6; 20:13, 14
22:13	Rev 1:8; 21:6; Isa 44:6; 48:12; Rev 1:17; 2:8; Rev 21:6
22:14	Gen 2:9; 3:22; Ezek 47:12; Rev 22:2, 19
22:15	1 Cor 6:9-10; Rev 21:8, 27
22:16	Isa 11:1, 10; Rom 1:3; Rev 5:5; Num 24:17; Rev 2:28
22:17	Isa 55:1; John 7:37; Rev 21:6
22:18-19	Deut 4:2; 12:32
22:19	Gen 2:9; 3:22; Ezek 47:12; Rev 22:2, 14
22:20	Rev 2:16; 3:11; 22:7, 12

However, if we situate the seer in the sky, thanks to his altered state of consciousness, we can begin with what the seer tells us explicitly about his sighting of the sky city, the new Jerusalem, in 21:1-27. This segment of the book offers two scenes: the first, an introduction, describes a new cosmos and the underlying theme of newness (21:1-5). The second scene describes the new Jerusalem (21:9-27). These two scenes are divided by a statement of moral encouragement (21:6-8), whose motivational force derives from a list of those who will and will not participate in these forthcoming realities. First, the introduction:

> 21:1. And I saw a new sky and a new earth; for the first sky and the first earth went away, and the sea no longer is. 2. And I saw the holy city, the new Jerusalem, coming down from the sky from God, prepared as a bride adorned for her husband. 3. And I heard a loud voice from the throne saying, "Behold the tent of God with men, and he will tent with them, and they will be his people, and he will be God with them, [their God]. 4. And he will wipe away every tear from their eyes, and death will be no longer, nor grief, nor wailing, nor will pain be any longer; [because] the first things went away." 5. And the one seated on the throne said: "Behold I make all things new"; and he said: "Write that: These are trustworthy and truthful utterances."

In this passage the seer beholds what looks like a fully decked-out Middle Eastern bride descending from the sky. Right at the outset he identifies it as part of God's remodeling effort, according to which God puts in a new sky and a new land. The cosmic sea is removed in the remodeling. Ancient geographers frequently depicted the habitable land, the *oikoumenē* as surrounded by an impassable sea (see Figure 1 above and the maps in the Loeb edition of Strabo, *Geography*). This sea remained from the original chaos of creation, when "the spirit moved over the face of the waters" (Gen 1:2). The sea often symbolizes chaos and death, and the separation of humans from God and the good things of paradise. No more death means no more cosmic sea and the restoration of God's presence along with the tree of life. Now the author inserts a promise coupled with a threat:

> 21:6. And he said to me: "It has happened. I [am] the Alpha and the O[mega], the beginning and the end. I will give the one thirsting from the source of living water for free. 7. The one conquering will inherit these things, and I will be God to him and he will be to me a son. 8. But to the timid and untrustworthy and filthy and murderers and fornicators and magic-practitioners and idolaters and all liars, their share [is] in the pit burning with fire and sulphur; this is the second death."

After this introduction and exhortation, the seer now gets down to describing the circumstances of how he got to see the sky city and, implicitly, why he thought it was a city that he saw:

> 21:9. And one of the seven sky servants having the seven bowls filled with the seven last injuries came and spoke with me saying: "Come here! I will show you the Bride, the Wife of the Lamb." 10. And he carried me up in sky wind over a great and high mountain, and he showed me the holy city Jerusalem coming down out of the sky from God, 11. having the glory of God; her brilliance like a most precious stone, as a crystalline jasper stone, 12. having a great and high wall, having twelve gates, and over the gates twelve sky servants, and names inscribed which are the twelve tribes of the sons of Israel. 13. From the east three gates, and from the north three gates, and from the south three

gates and from the west three gates. 14. And the wall of the city having twelve foundations, and upon these twelve the names of the twelve apostles of the Lamb. 15. And the one speaking with me had a golden measuring reed, so that he might measure the city and her gates and her walls. 16. The city was a quadrangle, and her length as much as her breadth. And he measured the city with the reed, twelve thousand stadia; her length and breadth and height were equal. 17. And he measured her wall, one hundred forty four cubits in human measure, that is sky servant (dimensions). 18. And the construction of her wall [was] jasper, and the city [was] pure gold like clear glass. 19. The foundations of the wall of the city [were] adorned all with precious stone; the first foundation jasper, the second sapphire, the third chalcedony, the fourth emerald, 20. the fifth sardonyx, the sixth sard, the seventh chrysolite, the eighth beryl, the ninth topaz, the tenth chrysoprasos, the eleventh hyacinth, the twelfth amethyst. 21. And the twelve gates twelve pearls, each of the gates was of one pearl. And the square of the city [was] pure gold, as lucid glass.

The author finally begins his description of the descending sky bride. The tradition of Isaiah 2:2 would have the new Jerusalem come down upon a mountain, perhaps on the very mountain on which the seer stood to get a better view of the descending sky city. This mountain seems to be one of the seven mountains found beyond the circle of the sea surrounding the *oikoumenē* (as in Figure 1 above). It is the mountain on which one finds the tree of life, on which God was found to be enthroned when he came to earth.

This mountain is now transposed to the center of the inhabited world, the *oikoumenē*. In Isaiah the temple of Jerusalem is often described as being located on "the mountain of the Lord" or on "my holy mountain" (Isa 11:9; 25:6-7, 10; 27:13; 30:29; 40:9; 56:7; 57:13; 65:11, 25; 66:20). But early on for this prophet, the mountain grows so high that it can be seen from any place in the *oikoumenē*: "It shall come to pass in the latter days that the mountain of the house of the Lord shall be established as the highest of the mountains, and shall be raised above the hills; and all the nations shall flow to it" (Isa 2:2). Von Rad (1966) suggested that the reconstituted Jesus-movement group addressed in the Sermon on the Mount is this mountain: "the city on the hill" of Matthew 5:14

(Greek: "city on the mountain"). This image conflates readily with Revelation. This exceedingly lofty mountain, towering above all mountains, finally realizes what Jerusalem was meant to be in hindsight. The tiny hill of Mount Moriah, on which Jerusalem's temple was built, is now an unbelievably high and huge mountain, unique in its kind, upon which is perched an unbelievably large city.

To get a better view, a familiar sky servant moves the seer up as high as possible toward the sky. Now he describes what he sees coming down. This "holy city Jerusalem coming down out of the sky from God" first of all alludes to the traditional Near Eastern view that deities had cities in the sky. The astral prophet Ezekiel also knew of this Jerusalem in the sky, although his wondrously gigantic mountain of observation in Israel (Ezek 40:2) enables him to see the city spread out before him (Ezek 40–48). Similarly, some seer at Qumran described visions of some forthcoming new Jerusalem (2Q 24; 4Q 554–555; 5Q 15; 11Q 18; see Chyutin 1994; for the temple presumably in this city, see 11Q 19–20 and Yadin 1983). In both Qumran and John, the exquisitely minute measurements of all dimensions of the city point to astronomical/astrological interests.

It seems that John knew that it was a city that he saw because of its walls and gates. While not all cities had walls and gates, any extremely large area surrounded by extremely large walls pierced by extremely large gates had to be a city. The prominence given to precious stones indicates that it is a sky city (see Tob 13:16-17), since all precious stones are intimately related to celestial bodies and vice versa (Rev 21:11, 18-21). The precious stones likewise point to a city of traditional Middle Eastern character. For example, as early as Hittite temple building, precious stones were part of the construction process.

> When they rebuild a temple that had been destroyed or (build) a new house in a different place and they lay the foundation . . . . Beneath the four corner(stones), each one of them, he deposits as follows:
> 1 foundation stone of silver,
> 1 foundation stone of gold,
> 1 foundation stone of lapis lazuli,

1 foundation stone of jasper,
1 foundation stone of marble,
1 foundation stone of iron,
1 foundation stone of copper,
1 foundation stone of bronze,
1 foundation stone of diorite.
The four corner(stones) are (each) provided with these in the same way (Goetz 1969: 356).

Furthermore, the fact that names of Israel's twelve tribes are inscribed over the guarded gates points to the sight as a new Jerusalem (Rev 21:12).

There can be little doubt that the new Jerusalem descending from the sky is an astral phenomenon. The city is of astronomical proportions, since it measures 12,000 stadia in length, width, and height. It is a cube, each side of which is the length of the Great Wall of China. Pliny notes: "A Greek stadion equals one hundred twenty-five of our Roman paces, that is six hundred twenty-five feet." (That is about 200 yards or 190 meters; *Natural History,* II, 21, 85, LCL; consider: a stadion = 607 feet; so 12,000 stadia come to 7,284,000 feet, or 1,380 miles.) This great cube would cover half of the United States and reach to the height of 260 Mount Everests (the top of Mount Everest stands 29,028 feet above sea level). Furthermore, the city was of transparent gold, "gold like pure crystal."

That the city is a cube fits the fundamental doctrine of astrology/astronomy concerning the regular figures in the zodiac. John's measurements begin with the note that its surface is a square, "its length is the same as its breadth" (Rev 21:16). In astral mathematics, the square designates the four "corners of the world" or the four directions of the sky. For the ancients, the square was an ideal form, an image of completion and perfection (see Plato, *Protagoras,* 344A; Aristotle, *Rhetoric,* III, 11, 2: a good man is "square," LCL). Pythagoreans treated the square and the cube as perfect mathematical figures playing a decisive role in how the world was constructed and maintained in harmony (see Aristotle, *Physics,* 4, 203a, 10). In the tradition of the Jerusalem sanctuary, the square was also an image of holiness, for the layout of the temple precinct was a square (see 1 Kgs 6 and the diagrams and bibliography in Metzger 1996). The holy of holies, on the other hand, was a set of squares forming a cube. And this city, too, was a cube: "its length, breadth and height are equal." If the square symbolizes holiness or purity, the cube symbolizes heightened holiness (hence holy of holies).

The cube is the well-known mathematical shape that designates the earth (Plato, *Timaeus,* 55, where fire matches the pyramid; water, the icosahedron; air, the octahedron; and the cosmos, the do-decahedron; in this arrangement the cube stands at the center of the dodecahedron). Thus this astronomically gigantic cube can readily be designated "the new earth." This city is laid out in the four direc-tions of the sky, just like the twelve signs of the zodiac. The fact that the city has no temple and no sun or moon for light points to a celestial arrangement above the present earth, sun, and moon. And the fact that twelve sky servants stand over its twelve gates is not unlike the twelve gates at the four corners of the cosmos through which winds and stars emerge (for example, 1 Enoch 33–35).

The repeated references to sets of twelve in the dimensions of the city (144 [12 x 12] ells for the wall, the twelve gates and their twelve angels, and then the twelve gemstones for the foundations) would exactly fit a scenario involving the twelve zodiacal constel-lations surrounding a central place consisting of the city and its central place, the throne of God and the Lamb (21:21). This twelvefold orientation is further replicated in the reference to the twelve tribes of the sons of Israel (21:12) and the twelve names of the twelve apostles of the Lamb (21:14), indicating that the Jesus Messiah group now coincides with Israel!

Twelve also ties in with the gemstones (see Söllner 1998: 221–223). In the Israelite tradition, we learn of such gemstones laid out in a square on the breastplate of the high priest of Israel from Exodus 28:17-20. Each of the stones on this breastplate was inscribed with the name of an Israelite tribe. The construction of the whole, in fact, related to the zodiac, as Josephus observed: "As for the twelve stones, whether one would prefer to read in them the months or the constellations of like number, which the Greeks call the circle of the zodiac, he will not mistake the lawgiver's inten-tion" (*Antiquities* III, 7, 7, 186, LCL). The gemstone substructure of the new Jerusalem was likewise part of Israelite tradition: "For Jerusalem will be built with sapphires and emeralds, her walls with precious stones, and her towers and battlements with pure gold. The streets of Jerusalem will be paved with beryl and ruby and stones of Ophir; all her lanes will cry 'Hallelujah!'" (Tob 13:16-18). In John's vision, the new and distinctive feature has to do with the names inscribed on the gemstones. For now it is the names of the twelve apostles of the Lamb that are etched on the gemstones forming the twelve foundations of the city.

Granted that the descending new Jerusalem is of astronomical proportions, what is the significance of this bride of the Lamb, the new Jerusalem, having the shape of an unbelievably huge, transparent, golden cube? In Israel's tradition, as previously noted, there is only one golden cube mentioned—the holy of holies of Solomon's temple (1 Kgs 6). Here that holy of holies has become a cosmic city, and the cosmic city a cosmic holy of holies. The new Jerusalem shaped as a cube of cosmic proportions is therefore an image of the new earth become the dwelling place of God. In Revelation 21:1-5 the new Jerusalem and the new earth are identical. The mathematics and geometric forms of 21:16-17 indicate that the city is a new holy of holies, the image of heightened holiness. Hence this new Jerusalem is "the holy city" (21:2).

As the figure representing the earth, the cosmic cube likewise points to the new Jerusalem as the new earth, the equivalent of perfection and harmony (as noted in 21:4-5). In ancient theory, the cube equally symbolizes perfect beauty; hence the new Jerusalem is likened to the beauty of an "adorned bride" (21:2). And as the proper locus of the presence of God in the holy of holies, the city is designated as temple (*skēnē,* literally "tent"), the place of the presence of God: "And God himself will be with them" (21:3). This statement clearly expresses what is distinctive about the new Jerusalem and hence the conspicuously salient quality of the new earth. All the other descriptive features of this final city are subordinate to the presence of God.

Thus the allusion to the shape of the holy of holies makes it obvious that there would be no temple in the city, since the cube city itself serves as the holy of holies.

21:22. And I did not see a temple in her, for the Lord God, the Almighty, is her temple, and the Lamb. 23. And the city has no need of the sun or the moon to illuminate her, for the glory of God lit her up, and the Lamb was her lamp. 24. And the nations walked about on account of her light; and the kings of the earth brought their glory into her. 25. And her gates surely would not be closed by day, for there was no night there. 26. And they will bring the glory and the honor of the nations into her. 27. And surely anything unclean and making an abomination or a lie would not enter into her, but only those written in the scroll of life of the Lamb.

While allusions to Isaiah 60 are apparent in this passage, it is important to note once more that the temple was the characteristic structure of the ancient Middle Eastern city. It seems that all cities of the region were built up around some initial temple belonging to a single god. Those temples or shrines without cities were really cities in abeyance (e.g., Beth-El, Beth Shan, Beth Shemesh, Beth Lehem, etc.). The world was managed by the gods, who decided on the function of things by "decreeing their fates," basically right after the separation of the sky and the land.

Temples in antiquity were not places of worship; rather they were residences for the gods, conceived as celestial, regional elites. The great gods, like great men, wished to be honored and served. So they created a first generation of cosmic beings, lesser gods (sons of gods, holy ones) to serve them. But a good number of these holy ones rebelled against the gods. In return, the gods created human beings for their service. "Kingship was lowered from the sky" in order to coordinate human efforts in the service of the gods (Wiggermann 1995: 1859). As the dictum had it: "The king is the last of the gods as a whole, but the first of human beings" (*Corpus Hermeticum III,* Fragment XXIV, 3, Nock-Festugière, 53). Whatever earthly kings had by way of staff—viziers, palace staff, army, tax collectors, etc.—so did the gods after whom the kings patterned themselves.

> To supply gods with their needs was the only purpose of the state and the justification for its survival; to do so was an obligation that could not be avoided. Avoidance was high treason;

> it jeopardized peace, prosperity, and life. The cult provided the
> gods with shelter and food or, in cultic terms, with a temple
> and offerings. . . . To serve the gods properly, the temple was
> equipped with a household (Wiggerman 1995: 1861).

The whole city itself was a temple, with God resident in the city
(21:22), perhaps with the Lamb serving as the ark of the covenant in the city shaped like the holy of holies (see Charles 1920:
ad versum). Noteworthy is the total lack of landscape forms and
the celestial phenomena that influenced old Jerusalem. There is
no mention of planetary influence, the stars, and atmospheric
phenomena marking agricultural seasons, the constellations
peering down upon the earthly culturescape, and the deities who
controlled all these. All these items were organically connected
to the people and place that constituted the old Jerusalem. In
other words, persons were organically tied to places by birth,
various family events, ancestors, and features of the place, such
as water, air, and sky events (see Malina 1993a). The emergence
of the new Jerusalem points to the end of such ethnic ties (to
kin, land, and water) as primary factors in the people's relationship to God.

In the new creation the sources of the earth's light (the daytime
and the moon) and warmth (the sun) are no longer needed, since
the glory of God and the Lamb provides the required climate.
Henceforth the sun and moon are no longer necessary to mark the
meaning of change, times, and seasons. The Lamb now does this,
serving as a new cosmic sign for everything needed by humans
who dwell on the land (21:23).

The new Jerusalem is, uniquely, a true terminal, totally and entirely centripetal. As the single central place in the new creation,
all persons, represented by their ruling regents, move to the city
with their glory (21:24, 26). Cities usually had guards at their
gates, and at night the gates were closed for protection. But now,
with the constant illumination, the need for closing the city at
night was not necessary. Now the constant illumination provided
by God's glory provides the security that locked gates usually did
(21:25).

Little is said about the inhabitants of the city other than that they include "only those written in the scroll of life of the Lamb." Those on this scroll make up the residents of the new and final city. These residents are those who submit to God. Thus residence is denied the unclean, the abominable, and liars or deceivers (21:27), previously listed as "the timid and untrustworthy and the filthy and murderers and fornicators and magic-practitioners and idolaters and all liars, their share [is] in the pit burning with fire and sulphur; this is the second death" (21:8).

This description presents the generic features of the sky city: bejeweled, unbelievably huge, duly walled and with gates, permanently illuminated like a sky object, having its times determined by the Lamb, duly populated by those enrolled by the Lamb and the centripetal "dead-end" (in fact the living terminal) of all humankind. As in all cities, there are some segments of the population perpetually excluded from the city and consigned to the "pit burning with fire and sulphur," the holy city's refuse dump. The author now turns to some specific features of the city.

> 22:1. And he showed me a river of water of life, resplendent as crystal, come out of the throne of God and of the Lamb. 2. In the middle of her square and of the river on the one side and the other a tree of life making twelve fruits, according to the month each giving its fruit, and the leaves of the tree for healing the nations. 3. And every curse will be no longer. And the throne of God and of the Lamb will be in her, and his slaves will worship him. 4. And they shall look upon his face and his name [will be] on their forehead. 5. And night will be no longer, and they will have no need of the light of a lamp and the light of the sun, because the Lord God will shine upon them and will reign into the aeons of aeons.

We are first told of the fact that the city has a river flowing through it, a river with crystal-clear water of life (22:1). The city has a square with trees. As with the tree of life in paradise of old that needed to be eaten by the earthling and his wife to maintain them in endless life (Gen 2:16), the trees around the square are trees of life (22:2). The water of life and the trees of life presumably nourish those living in the city in their endless existence. Only God is essentially immortal; humans need to drink and eat of whatever sources provide them with continued life. In case of illness, the leaves of the trees of life work equally well. The effects of curses cease; people are freed from the control of those entities that carry out curses.

The author repeats some information about the presence of the throne of God, the Lamb and the elimination of night (22:3-5), and adds a few details about the population. First of all, there are no citizens here—this is not a Greco-Roman *polis,* even of an imperial sort. Rather, the residents of this sky city are "slaves," tattooed with the name of the Lord, upon whose countenance they may gaze as they show reverence to God. In the first-century world, slavery was an act of dishonor, whether self-inflicted or done by others, consisting in depriving a person of freedom of decision and action by means of force or enforced solidarity with a view to the social utility of the slaveholder. Slavery was a form of social death in that enslaved persons lost the social status they previously had and could aspire to. Here, on the other hand, in the new Jerusalem we find a total reversal of the significance of that institution, for now being a slave of God was an act of honor enabling persons to serve God with strengthened freedom of decision and action in this service. It meant new social life, with status higher than that to which a person could ever aspire.

God, in turn, radiantly gazes upon the residents of the city (22:3-4). Life for the residents of this sky city come into being is one of euphoric and endless ecstasy. The experience of limited good has ceased (see Malina 1993b: 90–116). The author says nothing about other social dimensions of life in the city. Yet we know that cities in antiquity offered their elite residents and retainers in antiquity a set of desirable features, such as security at night (by closing gates); gate guards; congenial companionship; a different quality of life for non-elites to gaze on; the use of non-elites to serve as clients for elites, provide an entourage, and give honor; and finally, social security in the status quo. While ancient cities also included a whole set of persons not allowed to reside within, a set of permanent outcasts is also present in this sky-city scenario ("dogs," magicians, fornicators, murderers, idolaters, and the notable liars—22:15).

We are given some information about the city's ingroup and outgroup relations in the concluding portion of the book:

> 22:14. How honorable are those washing their garments so that their authority will be over the tree of life and [so that] they enter through the gates into the city. 15. Outside are the dogs and the magicians and the fornicators and the murderers and the idolaters and everyone loving and doing the lie.

Those who have access to the tree of life by entering through the gates of the city are "those washing their garments" (22:14). For the third time we are told of the outgroup: dogs, magicians, fornicators, murderers, idolaters, and liars (22:15). What all lists have in common is concern with liars, the final and emphasized category in the lists of the excluded (see Pilch 1994).

With this the description of the heavenly Jerusalem comes to a close. The book concludes with a number of directives and exhortations for those who receive "the prophecy of this scroll, for the time is near. Let the unjust behave unjustly still, and let the filthy practice filth still, and the just do justice still, and let the holy practice holiness still" (22:10-11).

Yet life at present really counts, since participation in the forthcoming city is God's recompense; God will "pay back each one according as their work is" (22:12). Those who are "washing their garments" will be duly honored, for "their authority will be over the tree of life and [so that] they enter through the gates into the city" (22:14). On the other hand, those not found worthy to enter will have to remain outside the city: "Outside are the dogs and the magicians and the fornicators and the murderers and the idolaters and everyone loving and doing the lie" (22:15). We also learn that if anyone tampers with this book of prophecy, "God will take away his share of the tree of life and of the holy city written in this scroll" (22:19).

Before the letter-ending of the work, the cosmic Jesus who appeared at the opening of the book once more informs its audience that he is "the root and the offspring of David, the brilliant

Morning Star," and that he sends this book with the description of
the events witnessed by the prophet to the churches (22:16). Fi-
nally, we are invited to join the Spirit and the Bride in urging the
Lamb of God to inaugurate the celestial wedding celebration:
"The Spirit and the Bride say, 'Come.' And let him who hears say,
'Come'" (22:17).

6. Some Conclusions About the Celestial City

The author does not tell us whether or not there are other cities
coexisting with the new Jerusalem. Yet he does emphasize that the
celestial Jerusalem is a unique entity, a focal cosmic reality for all
humankind. As a city, it is the centripetal central place in a network
of all humanity. To be some place can only be assessed in terms of
relationship to this central place. There is no other place that
counts. With the emergence of the celestial Jerusalem, we move
away from the old Jerusalem as a central seat of Judah and Israel
to Jerusalem as a central place of humankind.

What is this city intended to do? To begin with, if we look at
social relations, the author tells us that the city houses a throne.
From this we learn that it is a royal city of sorts, the seat of
power. Then we are told that the one seated on the throne is God,
indicating that the political structure expressed by the city is a
theocracy, a veritable kingdom of God. The simple mention of
God does not imply that the God in question is a cosmic, universal God, for it may be some local entity like the traditional
Middle Eastern deities. If this were a local God, the God of Israel, then the celestial Jerusalem would simply be a replay of the
old Jerusalem.

We are told that there is a Lamb equally centered on the throne.
If the Lamb is simply Israel's Messiah, we have another indication
that the city is a replay of old Jerusalem. But if this Lamb is the
cosmic Lamb, the veritable Lamb of God that makes the seasons
change in their rotation and that leads and controls the zodiacal
procession of constellations, then we have a cosmic orientation
with cosmic power at a cosmic center. The God in question is the

universal God of all, while the Lamb is in fact the *polokrator,* the controller of all the entities that constitute the sky.

The book of John's revelation thus turns out to be much concerned with God's celestial Jerusalem as the central place of humankind. Why would John pick Jerusalem? Why not a heavenly Rome or any other city? What made it possible for him to pick Jerusalem as the central place for humankind?

As sole city descending from the sky, the new Jerusalem is the terminal city par excellence. All roads necessarily lead to it. And as sole city, all humanity forms an ingroup with the city and its regent at the hub. It is the final terminal, the center of the ingroup, the place to which every other feature of the human network connects. It thus becomes the center of life in the *oikoumenē,* and for all practical purposes, the center of life on earth. The God who descends and resides in the city is now "our" God, not just the God of Israel. This main and sole God of the celestial city is the terminal God of the cosmos. As central and unique city, this Jerusalem is no longer an Israelite phenomenon. The one speaking or dealing with Jerusalem in the book of Revelation is revealed to be the Alpha and Omega, the Beginning and End of all peoples. And as Ezekiel's final words noted, the name of this new city is no longer Jerusalem, but "the name of the city henceforth shall be: 'Yahweh is there'" (Ezek 48:35).

It is thus acquisition by the sole God of the city and loyalty to the sole God that constitute basis for residence in the city. This marks a change from the prevalent belief in social territoriality: that people are organically linked to the land of their origin, its gods, its society, and the like. It seems that Rome's Hellenistic conception of Roman citizenship, dependent not on ethnicity and/or residence but invested in individual affiliation and loyalty, resonates here. "The conclusion is that at Rome any connection between citizenship and ethnicity was attenuated to the point where it was practically nonexistent" (Cornell 1991: 65).

With Roman citizenship invested in individuals regardless of ethnicity, the boundaries of Rome move to wherever its citizens are. The result is a social experience that might serve as ready analogy for a deity beyond ethnic affiliation. This social feature allows for the development and replication of the idea and conception of a universal polity and a universal deity for all people, regardless of ethnicity. In terms of political religion, what counts now is belonging to a network of dependable and loyal slaves of God acting in terms of allegiance to the only deity enthroned in an earthly city descended from the sky.

In antiquity, faith never meant faith in the existence of God or gods. Faith always meant loyalty to one of a number of high deities, some single, ultimate entity that was believed to control one's existence. John the prophet distinctively reports that there is only one single high God, once enthroned and resident in the sky above Jerusalem but soon to be located in the single, central city towering above everything in the created world, a city in fact that would be the new earth. There are no other gods in the sky or on earth. This is monotheism, expressed so clearly perhaps for the first time by anyone in the Israelite tradition, now outfitted with new lenses deriving from the experience of the resurrected Jesus.

From the viewpoint of the gospel focused on Christ Jesus, it is very obvious that the emerging and descending celestial Jerusalem, now the residence of God and the Lamb with earthlings, is God's central, essential, total proclamation effort. The outcome of the emergence of this city is the streaming of Israelites and Gentiles to God (Isa 2:2: "all the nations shall flow to it"; Isa 66:20: "And they shall bring all your brethren from all the nations"). The city marks God attracting all persons in the renewed *oikoumenē*. This is God as perceived in Jesus-group experience, the one who does the calling of people to himself (e.g., Rom 1:7; 8:28; 11:29; 1 Cor 1:2, 9, 24; 1 Thess 2:12; also 1 Pet 5:10).

Jesus similarly saw his task in Israel to be a harvesting operation (Matt 9:38; Luke 10:2; even John 4:38 and Paul in Rom 1:13). Paul, in turn, saw his task among his fellow Israelites in the Judean colonies as one of proclaiming, making known what happened in Jerusalem so that his fellow ethnics would come in of themselves (Rom 10:14-15). This likewise characterized the perception of God as the one who took the initiative in outreach to Gentiles in the book of Acts (10:1-33). It is always God who does the calling, the attracting.

Israel's prophets, too, noted how the emergence of the city itself triggers or sets off the coming of all peoples to God, even if, in their own ethnocentric way, for the service of Israel. This of course is a central feature of the theology of the book of Revelation. The task of wandering apostles seems to have been to set up conditions so that people might be able to hear the call of God and follow the attraction that God embodies.

4

The Cosmic Lamb Marries

In this final chapter we shall first consider the cosmic Lamb and its significance for humankind, and then the wedding of the Lamb and the celestial city. The Lamb is a celestial entity that appears in a number of scenes in the book of Revelation. The Lamb is not just any astral body but rather a highly exalted Lamb, presented early on in the book (Rev 5:6-8, 12-13; 6:1, 16; 7:9, 10, 14, 17; 8:1) and repeatedly described in terms of its significant activity (Rev 12:11; 13:8, 11; 14:1, 4, 10; 15:3; 17:14).

1. The Lamb of God

In the book of Revelation the cosmic Lamb is introduced as follows: "And I saw in the middle of the throne and of the four living beings and in the middle of the elders a lamb standing as though slaughtered, having seven horns and seven eyes, [which are the (seven) sky winds of God sent upon the whole earth]" (5:6). A significant clue to the identity of this Lamb is the fact that it is standing as though it had been slaughtered. In the hymn to this cosmic Lamb that shortly follows, it is described as the Lamb who "has been slaughtered" (5:9). These indications are sufficient

to point to the astral Lamb, the constellation known to Romans
and Greeks as Aries:

> The Latin and Greek names of this constellation (Latin: *Aries,*
> from Greek *Arēs,* lamb; and Greek: *Krios* both used to mean
> "ram") are rather recent. The traditional name of this zodiacal
> being (Phoenician: *Teleh,* Israelite: *Tale>,* Arabic: *Al-Hamal*)
> was "Male Lamb." From time immemorial, Aries was always
> pictured in the most ancient representations of the sky as a
> male lamb with a "reverted" head, that is as facing directly over
> its back to Taurus. Thus Manilius describes Aries in his poem:
> "Resplendent in his golden fleece, first place holder Aries looks
> backward admiringly at Taurus rising" (Manilius, *Astronomica*
> 1.263–264, LCL). Only a being with a broken neck could have
> its head turned directly backwards as the celestial Aries does;
> and yet it remains standing in spite of the broken neck. Clearly,
> Aries was an obvious choice to be perceived in terms of the
> Christian story according to which God's Lamb was slaugh-
> tered yet continues to stand (Malina 1995: 78–79).

The prominence and eminence of the cosmic Lamb simply cannot
be too highly emphasized. For this Lamb is the first of all constellations, the first created celestial body marking the inauguration
of the cosmos:

> Aries (the Ram) is the first in the zodiac, the center and head of
> the cosmos as the astrologers say (see Boll 1914: 44, n. 2; there
> he cites Nigidius Figulus, first century A.D., who calls Aries "the
> leader and prince of the constellations"; the *Scholia in Aratum*
> 545, relating that "the Egyptians [Nechepso-Petosiris] say Aries
> is the head"; and Nonnos, who says that Aries "is the center of
> the whole cosmos, the central navel of Olympus"; Vettius Valens,
> Rhetorios and Firmicus Maternus are quite similar. Further, the
> Greek words for lamb, sheep, and ram are often used synony-
> mously, even in the same tradition. Boll (1914: 45, n. 6) cites the
> tradition of the "ram of Pelops" called variously lamb and sheep.
> And in Ps 113:4, 5, ram and lamb are used in parallel.
>
> Aries is the leader of the stars of the ecliptic: "The Wool-
> Bearer leads the signs for his conquest of the sea" (Manilius, *As-
> tronomica* 2.34, LCL). According to astrological lore that

focused on the zodiac and its ecliptic belt, at the beginning of the universe Aries stood in mid-heaven (Greek: *mesouranēma* is an astronomical technical term), that is, at the "head" of the cosmos, at the summit of it all. For example, Firmicus Maternus writes: "We must now explain why they began the twelve signs with Aries. . . . In the chart of the universe which we have said was invented by very learned men, the mid-heaven is found to be in Aries. This is because frequently—or rather, always—in all charts, the mid-heaven holds the principal place, and from this we deduce the basis of the whole chart, especially since most of the planets and the luminaries—the Sun and the Moon—send their influence toward this sign" (*Mathesis,* III, 1, 17–18, trans. Rhys Bram 75). Ancient Israel likewise recognized the prominence of Aries in its New Year celebration connected with its foundational event, the Exodus (Exod 12:2: the Exodus occurs in the first month of the year). And the ritual marking the Exodus involved a male lamb, Aries itself (Malina 1995: 102).

Among the learned of antiquity, it was common belief that when the cosmic Lamb reached its original position, that is, the sky location it occupied as it issued from the hands of God the creator, then the sky and earth would be renewed, made new. The significant detail in Revelation, as will be noted, is the fact that the wedding of the Lamb takes place at the point of origin of the zodiacal Aries, the cosmic Lamb. This, of course, fits the theme of newness very well, since Aries stands at the beginning of things.

When the vault of the sky returns to the position it had at the very time of creation, it will be with Aries at the point of pre-eminence, the head of the cosmos. And such a return to beginnings was expected. For people commonly measure the year by the circuit of the sun, that is, of a single star alone; but when all the stars return to the place from which they at first set forth, and, at long intervals, restore the original configuration of the whole heaven, then that can truly be called a revolving year. . . . I hardly dare to say how many generations of men are contained within such a year; for as once the sun appeared to men to be eclipsed and blotted out, at the time when the soul of Romulus entered these regions, so when the sun shall again be eclipsed at the same point and in the same season, you may be-

> lieve that all the planets and stars have returned to their original positions, and that a year has actually elapsed. But be sure that a twentieth part of such a year has not yet passed (Cicero, *The Republic,* VI, xxii, 24, LCL).

For Cicero, the "revolving year" refers to the so-called Great Year. According to Needham, the Greek tradition believed the Great Year to consist of thirty-six thousand solar years; at every Great Year events in the entire cosmos as well as on earth repeat themselves down to the minutest detail due to "resumption by the planets and constellations of their original places" (Needham 1981: 133). Belief in a Great Year is rooted in, and serves to support, the "image of limited good" that was quite prevalent in antiquity (Malina 1993b: 90–116). The same might be said for the Israelite speculative notion of "a world week of six epochs of 1,000 years each," with the close of the final thousand years marking the returning to the beginning (Rordorf 1968: 48). For our author, that year is already here with the wedding of the Lamb (Malina 1995: 240–241).

If the cosmic Lamb ushers in a new order with a new sky and a new land, the new beginning does away with everything that preceded. All previous accounts are set aside. The sin of the world, ways of living that disgrace or dishonor God, cease to be. The Lamb of God thus takes away the sin of the world just as light does away with darkness, just as life does away with death. The Lamb of God in John 1:29, 36 is one of the celestial titles of Jesus with which the Gospel opens: Word, Life, Light, Lamb of God, Son of God, Son of Man. Another title that seems earthly but really marks another link between the sky and the land is King of Israel. Kings are the lowest of the gods, the highest of humans. In the outlook of the day, "The king is the last of the gods as a whole, but the first of human beings" (*Corpus Hermeticum III,* Fragment XXIV, 3, Nock-Festugière, 53).

2. The Lamb and God's Plan for Humankind

In his description of his first trip to the sky, John tells of four constellations along the celestial equator and at opposite points from each other (Taurus, Leo, Scorpio-Man, and Pegasus, whom Mesopotamians called the Thunderbird—Rev 4:6-8). At the center of this arrangement was the constellation called the Throne, from which God exercised his power (this throne, of course, was in a celestial temple—Rev 7:15). And around the central throne were twenty-four enthroned and crowned star beings called "elders," a synonym for the astronomical term "decan" (see Gundel 1936a).

The problem posed in this opening experience was this: Who had enough cosmic honor to set loose God's plan for people in the land of Israel who refused to repent? The Lamb of God, the most worthy constellation Aries, identified with the Lion of Judah, steps forward and opens the scroll, seal by seal, resulting in the gradual destruction of the land of Israel, culminating at its central city, "where their Lord was crucified" (11:8). This opening scenario is balanced by a final scenario describing the emergence of the celestial Jerusalem at the close of the book (chaps. 20–21). In between we are given an astronomically based explanation for why life at present is the way it is: we are taken to the time before creation is completed when the dragon, Satan, is cast to earth (second scene). We then learn of the fate of the first city created by human beings after the Deluge, Babel-Babylon the great (third scene). Again, this first city of our era of humankind, that is, the first city of the postdiluvial period, finds its contrast with the final city, the celestial Jerusalem.

In many respects, then, the final emergence of Jerusalem from the sky is the high point of the book, alluded to repeatedly in what preceded (notably by the mention of God's temple in the sky: Rev 7:15; 11:2, 19; 14:15, 17; 15:5, 8; 16:1, 17). The first reference to this city comes in the opening edict to the Philadelphians:

> The one who conquers—I shall make him a pillar in the temple of my God, and he shall certainly no longer depart outside, and I shall write upon it [him] the name of my God and the name of the city of my God, the new Jerusalem which descends out of the sky from my God, and my new name (Rev 3:12).

But the first implicit allusion to the approaching appearance of this city is the announcement of the marriage of the Lamb, whose bride has made herself ready, and mention of a forthcoming wedding feast (19:9-10). It is only at the close of the book, however, that we learn that the bride is the holy city, the new Jerusalem, that it descends from God as a bride adorned for her husband (21:2), and that this city is, in fact, the cosmic bride destined to be the wife of the Lamb of God (21:9-10).

3. The Conjunction of the Cosmic Lamb and Sky City

As we have seen, the seer tells of his witnessing the emergence of a new sky and a new land, and of his vision of "the holy city, new Jerusalem, coming down out of the sky from God." But that is not all, for this new Jerusalem appears "prepared as a wife adorned for her husband" (21:1-2). Why the reference to a descending celestial city married to a cosmic Lamb? There is, in fact, a constellation known to the ancients as "The Wedding of the Gods," which is located in the vicinity of Cancer.

> "The Wedding of the Gods" was part of traditional Egyptian sky lore and is duly noted in a book called *The Book of Hermes Trismegistus,* published by Gundel (1936b), a sixth century A.D. Latin version of a work deriving from an original Egyptian writing from the Ptolemaic period (see Festugière 1950: 112–123). The constellation is likewise mentioned in a Greek text published by Franz Cumont, where it bears the Greek name *theōn gamos,* that is, Wedding of the Gods (Cumont, *Catalogus Corpus Astrologicorum Graecorum* VIII/4, 119, 16, corrected by Cumont as noted by Gundel 1936b: 259). In *The Book of Hermes Trismegistus* this constellation is mentioned twice. First, the author has a list of all the stars and/or constellations that accompany the rising of the twelve zodiacal signs, noting at which of the thirty degrees assigned to each sign the given star or constellation is to be found. Under Cancer we read: "The twenty-ninth degree (of Cancer) is called the Wedding of the Gods"—*Vicesimus nonus gradus vocatur deorum nuptiae* (Gundel 1936b: 60, 1). We are further told that this location in the sky ranks as "vacant," hence neither negative nor positive in its influence on the earth and its inhabitants! This agrees with a

prior mention of this constellation in a general section explaining how to interpret the sky. There the compiler writes: "The final degrees of the zodiacal signs generally signify dishonorable qualities in one's mother except for the final degrees of Libra and Cancer. For the final degrees (of Libra) are called 'Increase,' and of Cancer, 'The Wedding of the Gods'" (Gundel 1936b: 41, 10–11), (Malina 1995: 239).

Gundel (1936b) has suggested that the lore behind this constellation derives from Egyptian tradition. It would have been something like what can be found in Plutarch's work on Isis and Osiris:

> Here follows the story related in the briefest possible words with the omission of everything that is merely unprofitable or superfluous: They say that the Sun, when he became aware of Rhea's intercourse with Cronus, invoked a curse upon her that she should not give birth to a child in any month or any year; but Hermes, being enamored of the goddess, consorted with her. Later, playing at draughts with the Moon, he won from her the seventieth part of each of her periods of illumination, and from all the winnings he composed five days, and intercalated them as an addition to the three hundred and sixty days. The Egyptians even now call these five days intercalated and celebrated them as the birthdays of the gods. They relate that on the first of these days Osiris was born, and at the hour of his birth a voice issued forth saying, "The Lord of All advances to the light." But some relate that a certain Pamyles, while he was drawing water in Thebes, heard a voice issuing from the shrine of Zeus, which bade him proclaim with a loud voice that a mighty and beneficent king, Osiris, had been born; and for this Cronus entrusted to him the child Osiris, which he brought up. It is in his honor that the festival of Pamylia is celebrated, a festival which resembles the phallic processions. On the second of these days Arueris was born whom they call Apollo, and some call him also the elder Horus. On the third day Typhon was born, but not in due season or manner, but with a blow he broke through his mother's side and leapt forth. On the fourth day Isis was born in the regions that are ever moist; and on the fifth Nephthys, to whom they give the name of Finality and the name of Aphrodite, and some also the name of Victory. There

is also a tradition that Osiris and Arueris were sprung from the Sun, Isis from Hermes, and Typhon and Nephthys from Cronus. For this reason the kings considered the third of the intercalated days as inauspicious and transacted no business on that day, nor did they give any attention to their bodies until nightfall. They relate, moreover, that Nephthys became the wife of Typhon; but Isis and Osiris were enamored of each other and consorted together in the darkness of the womb before their birth. Some say that Arueris came from this union and was called the elder Horus by the Egyptians, but Apollo by the Greeks (*Isis and Osiris* 12, 355D–356A, LCL).

The value of this information is that it demonstrates that there was in fact a constellation in the sky referred to as a Divine Wedding. There were celestial, astronomical weddings. Such a celestial configuration was available for first-century Eastern Mediterranean prophets to appropriate into their traditions.

The significant feature here, though, is that this wedding of the Lamb and the sky city is not a pre-existing constellation. It is an event soon to take place. Furthermore, it portends the transformation of creation into a new sky and a new land. How and why? The fact is that the very mention of the wedding of the Lamb with its celestial bride would clue the astute astral reader to the advent of the new sky and the new land. Non-constellational weddings are quite common in the sky, since stars, including planets, have their conjunctions. "Conjunction" (Latin: *coniunctio;* Greek: *súndesmos, súnodos, suzugía*) is the technical name for the overlapping or union of celestial bodies; it is equally a term for marital union, a "wedding," if you will (see Liddell-Scott, *ad verba*). Consequently, a celestial conjunction of the cosmic Lamb and the celestial city would be labeled a "wedding," albeit astronomical (see Figure 4). Since the celestial new Jerusalem "comes down out of the sky from God" (21:2), the sky location of the event is at the opening in the sky offering access to God's side of the vault of the sky. It is at this point in the sky that God launched the creation of the sky and earth. The fact that the Lamb is in conjunction with the city at the point where the Lamb began its cosmic career points to the onset of the cosmic (re)newal that the ancients expected.

The emergence of God's city from God's side of the sky and its descent toward the land below is signaled by the presence of the Lamb at the proper celestial location: the conjunction of the Lamb and the opening in the vault of the sky leading to the other side, God's side. The heavenly Jerusalem emerges from the opening in the sky, mentioned previously in the book of Revelation and variously in the Bible (1 Kgs 22:19; 2 Chr 18:18; Ezek 1:1; Mark 1:10; Matt 3:16; Rev 4:1). To get to God's real home in his celestial temple and its attendant city, a person had to pass through the opening in the firmament that led to the other side of the vault of the sky where the God in question was enthroned. In Mesopotamian lore, appropriated so well by Israel, this opening was to be found directly over God's earthly temple. In Acts, for example, the sky opens above Jerusalem to allow the resurrected Jesus to as-

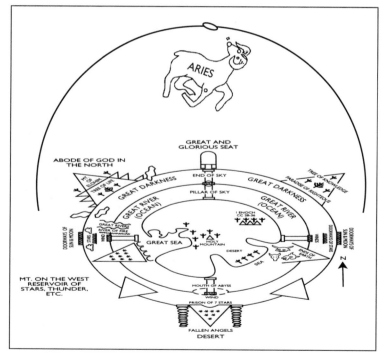

Figure 4: The "Marriage" of the Lamb and the City

cend to God, of course, through the opening in the firmament
(Acts 1:2-7). Likewise because of a sky opening, Stephen in Jerusalem can see the exalted Jesus standing by the throne of God
(Acts 7:56). And in Revelation, John frequently mentions this
opening and his seeing the ark of the covenant in the center of the
temple. This is consonant with Israel's tradition, according to
which certain people saw God's presence in the sky from earthly
Jerusalem. God's "holy habitation," his "dwelling place," is in the
sky (Deut 26:15; 1 Kgs 8:43; 2 Chr 30:27), high in the sky (Job
22:12); "he walks on the vault of the sky" (Job 22:14); hence he is
located beyond the vault, for he sits enthroned on high above the
stars, on the mythical Mountain of Assembly in the far north (Isa
14:13-14; 2 Chr 18:18). The prophet Micaiah "saw the LORD sit-
ting on his throne, and all the host of heaven standing on his right
hand and on his left" (1 Kgs 22:19; 2 Chr 18:18). Clearly his holy
temple, his throne, is in the sky (Ps 11:4), although he does have a
house at Jerusalem (2 Chr 36:23; Ezra 1:2).

Of course, John's interpretation of his experience is replete
with Israelite allusions. After all, John is an Israelite prophet in
the resurrected Jesus tradition. These allusions begin with his positioning at the remarkable mountain observatory (21:10, from
Ezekiel 40:2, Isaiah 2:2, and Israelite lore as in Enoch; see Buxton 1992) on which he finds himself studying the descending new
city. They continue with references to features of the city itself
(notably as in Ezekiel 40–44). As an astral prophet in the Jesus
tradition, John reads the traditional Middle Eastern skyscape
through Israelite lenses, newly polished and thus refocused by his
experience of the resurrected Jesus.

In subsequent interpretations of the sky by members of the resurrected Jesus tradition, the opening in the sky to God's realm
stands at the cosmic cross, the place where the celestial equator
and the belt of the zodiac intersect. This item of information was
well known in early Jesus groups (see Daniélou 1964: 265–292).
Whether the intimations in the book of Revelation were its first
expression or not we do not know; but here we have a conjunction
of the sky opening and the cosmic Lamb and the subsequent
emergence of the celestial city over the land chosen by God as the

place where God would be henceforth manifest. What John subsequently offers is a description of this sky city, in which the
throne of God is to be found along with the celestial Lamb. These
wedded celestial entities marked the inauguration of God's presence among men on the land.

4. The Celestial Wedding as Conclusion to the Book

Many Europeans and North Americans have problems with the
conclusion of the book of Revelation (e.g., Charles 1920; Flusser
1988: 455, n. 1 for a list). They expect it to come to a logical and
satisfactory denouement, a conclusion characteristic of the stories
that Europeans or North Americans tell, in terms of some logical
progression reaching to an end. A cursory reading of modern commentators who have dealt with the last chapters of Revelation
reveals how frequently the category "logical" fits into their presuppositions: it would be logical if . . . , it is more logical to consider
. . . , etc. The fact of the matter is that ancient books dealing with
the sky are never logical in terms of modern expectations. They are
essentially descriptions of sightings from specific perspectives. The
fact is that ancient sky compilers, ancient observers of the sky, did
not have much interest in logic. Their interest consisted in compil-
ing from one and all whatever observations anyone might have
made. Their work is cumulative, a conglomeration of whatever any
other duly credentialed observer has observed. They see a piece of
the sky, and what they see they set down.

Perceptions of the "fact" that the last chapters of Revelation do
not lead to a proper story ending, a logical conclusion, emerge
only during and after the Romantic period. As Prickett (1996) has
noted, it was due to Romanticism that biblical scholars started to
read the Bible as a story, a *Geschichte*. This is quite significant. It
was the novel genre that popularized among Romantic elites and
pathbreakers the perception of human social reality as based in
story, a story in which chronology, time sequence, emotional development, uniqueness really counted. (The "roman-" in Romantic comes from the French and German word for the "novel.")

Since the book of Revelation described the end, the end should be a satisfactory and logical conclusion to an unfolding story. It is the quest for a proper and logical story ending that moved many to rearrange the final chapters of Revelation. It is also this quest for a proper story that introduced salvation history and the perception of the Bible as one long story from creation to conclusion.

If we uncover what these passages meant to their original audience, perhaps their significance would be somewhat different. A logical story line was not the primary purpose; to describe relevant segments of the sky was. The primary purpose of Israelite astral prophecy as we find it in the book of Revelation is to describe what has occurred in segments of the sky of significance to John's audience in order to assure them of what must take place soon (1:1). In the meantime, they must not be deceived, a constant theme in the book.

The descent of the sky city of Jerusalem, even in Tertullian's time (d. 220), was taking place over the Roman province of Syria-Palestine. The sky Jerusalem would rest where the present destroyed Jerusalem now stands, and its message will necessarily lie enfolded in, and supported by, the situation of Judea. Thus Tertullian notes:

> This both Ezekiel had knowledge of (48:30-35) and the Apostle John saw (Rev 21:2). And the word of the new prophecy [Montanism] which is part of our belief attests how it foretold that there would be for a sign a picture of this very city exhibited to view previous to its manifestation. This prophecy, indeed, has been very lately fulfilled in an expedition to the East [Emperor Severus against the Parthians]. For it is evident from the testimony of even heathen witnesses, that in Judea there was suspended in the sky a city early every morning for forty days. As the day advanced, the entire fixture of its walls would wane gradually, and sometimes it would vanish instantly. We say that this city has been provided by God for receiving the saints on their resurrection (*Tertullian Against Marcion* 3, 24, 4, CCSL I: 542 and for the version ANF 3, 342–343).

In the same context, Tertullian attests that he believed Paul was speaking of this descending celestial reality in Galatians 4:26

with his reference to the Jerusalem that comes down from the sky, "the Jerusalem above (that) is free, (that) is our mother!" For it is the city in which the followers of Christ have their residential quarter with fellow Jesus-group members (the Latin-speaking Tertullian cites the Greek word *politeuma;* see Phil 3:20).

Conclusion

Does the foregoing interpretation provide adequate scenarios to make sense of the sky city and its wedding to the cosmic Lamb as presented by the author of the book of Revelation? The type of historical interpretation presented in this book is a historical approach rooted in a social-scientific perspective to biblical interpretation. The search for historical antecedents to what the author is doing, as well as their existence, has to be formulated into a model deriving from empirical data and empirical verification. The empirical data considered here have been provided by contemporary comparative urban studies and astronomical studies. These data and the models that produced them were borrowed and applied to documents from the past in order to explain those documents in a comparative way. In other words, models that explain what actually exists today are appropriated and historically attuned into models of the past, first by removing those obvious insertions that emerged over the past two thousand years and then by expanding what remains in dimensions consistent with the modern and ancient Mediterranean culture area. The process results in two sets of models—the one of the present, the other of the past—that provide points of comparison and serve as a touchstone for envisioning the past in some probable and verifiable way. This is more or less what historically based, social-scientific interpretation of the New Testament does. Among the hallmarks of the procedure we mention the following:

1. Definition of terms. Often the attempt to define terms points up problems that can only be solved by cross-cultural comparison. The terms of interest here were "city" and "marriage." Consider the confusion that surrounds undefined words such as "urban," "divorce," "conversion" now and in antiquity. The meanings of

undefined words are usually taken for granted by biblical scholars, yet those modern experiences labeled with these words have little in common with antiquity.

2. If something exists today, it is quite possible that it might have existed earlier, given adequate historical indications. In other words, if something exists, one might deduce its previous existence if this can be verified *(Ab esse ad posse valet illatio)*. Thus if Mediterranean peasants behave in a certain way today, they might have behaved that way in the past.

But the opposite perspective is considered totally inadequate in logic. Not a few interpreters believe that if something is possible, conceivable, or thinkable, it must have been! Thus if I can think of something in the past ("wasn't it possible?"), then it quite likely was that way. The fact is that biblical interpretation is rooted in the imagination of historians working with scenarios of unverifiable possibilities retrojected on antiquity. Consider all that has been written about Paul's addressees as "urban Christians," and the (modern) psychological stimuli that led them to behave the way they did! Or what is said about the fall of Rome as mirroring our social situation! At issue here are John's astral visions in an altered state of consciousness. Does the reality of such visions fit the modern Mediterranean? Does it fit the ancient Mediterranean? Alternate states of consciousness are to be found among 90 percent of the world's populations today (see Bourgignon 1973). The Enlightenment filtered out this dimension of human experience as irrational, and Western interpreters do not consider it an option in their works (see Pilch 1993).

3. From the definitions and principles, construct a model. Here we offered a general model of a city, with a comparative model of the Hellenistic and Middle Eastern city. A good model will have the following features:

a) It should be a cross-cultural model, accounting for the interpreter as well as those interpreted in some comparative perspective. To account for the modern city experience, nothing of modern city life is found in the comparison.

b) It should be of a sufficient level of abstraction to allow for the surfacing of similarities that facilitate comparison.

c) It should be able to fit a larger sociolinguistic frame for interpreting texts. The type of city emerging in the models can serve as a scenario for understanding documents from the past.

d) It should derive from experiences that match what we know of the time-and-place-conditioned biblical world as closely as possible. Here the model of the Middle Eastern city covers all the data about the sky city presented in John's Revelation.

e) The meanings the model generates should be understandable but irrelevant to people in our twentieth-century Western societies. All things being equal, irrelevant meanings have a higher probability of being true, given the step-level changes that have occurred since the first century.

f) The application of the model should be acceptable to social scientists (even if they disagree with the validity of the enterprise—they are often ignorant of history, theology, and the philosophical bases of their disciplines; most recently in this regard, see Coleman 1999).

The outcome of this approach to the Bible is an increased understanding of the people described in the scenes presented in New Testament documents. The scenes, of course, derive from the experiences of the persons who people the documents. They serve to delineate the behavior ascribed to God by analogy with human behavior. With this approach, instead of biblical dogmas, we come to know and appreciate the personages who embodied biblical faith. Instead of moral directives and theological propositions, we discover social persons and the underpinnings of their interpersonal relations. Instead of the biblical basis and source of the "religion of the book," we would find the Bible as a reflection of the "religion of persons" and their theocentric and christocentric successes and failures that lie at the source of Christian tradition. Instead of abstract theology, we make the acquaintance of our flesh-and-blood Christian ancestors in faith and the dimensions of their quest for an adequately meaningful human existence. In this way one presumably fulfills the primary task of exegetes: to find out what biblical documents meant to their initial, Mediterranean audiences.

Abbreviations

AJPh	*American Journal of Philology*
ANF	Ante-Nicene Fathers
BAR	*Biblical Archaeology Review*
CCSL	Corpus Christianorum Scriptorum Latinorum
CJ	*Classical Journal*
CSSH	*Comparative Studies in Society and History*
ILS	*Inscriptiones Latinae Selectae*
JSNT	*Journal for the Study of the New Testament*
JSOT	*Journal for the Study of the Old Testament*
LCL	Loeb Classical Library
TANZ	Texte und Arbeiten zum neutestamentlichen Zeitalter
TAPA	*Transactions of the American Philological Association*

Bibliography

Abu-Lughod, Janet
    1975   "Comments on the Form of Cities: Lessons from the Islamic City." In *Janus: Essays in Ancient and Modern Studies,* edited by Louis L. Orlin, 119–130. Ann Arbor: Univ. of Michigan Press.

    1976   "The Legitimacy of Comparisons in Comparative Urban Studies: A Theoretical Position and an Application to North African Cities." In *The City in Comparative Perspective: Cross-National Research and New Directions in Theory,* edited by John Walton and Louis H. Masotti, 17–43. New York: Sage/Wiley.

Albertz, Rainer
    1994   *A History of Israelite Religion in the Old Testament Period.* Trans. John Bowden. Louisville: Westminster/John Knox Press.

Anderson, Albert
    1983   "The Culture of the Greek Polis: The Unified View of Plato and Aristotle." In *Aspects of Greco-Roman Urbanism: Essays on the Classical City,* edited by Ronald T. Marchese, 42–60. BAR International Series 188. Oxford: BAR.

Atherton, Patrick
    1986   "The City in Ancient Religious Experience." In *Classical Mediterranean Spirituality,* edited by A. Armstrong, 314–336. New York: Crossroads.

Aune, David E.
    1997–1999   *Revelation*. Word Biblical Commentary 52a–c. Dallas: Word Books.

Barraclough, Geoffrey
    1978   *Main Trends in History*. New York and London: Holmes and Meier.

Bauckham, Richard
    1993   *The Theology of the Book of Revelation*. Cambridge: Cambridge Univ. Press.

Boatwright, M. T.
    1986   "The Pomerial Extension of Augustus." *Historia* 35: 13–27.

Boll, Franz
    1967   *Sphaera: Neue griechische Texte und Untersuchungen zur Geschichte der Sternbilder*. 1903. Reprint, Hildesheim: Georg Olms.

    1967   *Aus der Offenbarung Johannis: Hellenistische Studien zum Weltbild der Apokalypse*. Leipzig and Berlin, 1914. Reprint, Amsterdam: Hakkert.

Bourguignon, Erika
    1973   *Religion, Altered States of Consciousness, and Social Change*. Columbus: Ohio State Univ. Press.

Bowman, A. K., and D. Rathbone
    1992   "Cities and Administration in Roman Egypt." *Journal of Roman Studies* 82: 107–127.

Boyd, Thomas D., and Michael H. Jameson
    1981   "Urban and Rural Land Division in Ancient Greece." *Hesperia* 50: 327–342.

Burnell, Peter J.
    1992   "The Status of Politics in St. Augustine's City of God." *History of Political Thought* 13: 13.

Burns, Alfred
    1976   "Hippodamus and the Planned City." *Historia* 25: 414–428.

Buxton, Richard
    1992   "Imaginary Greek Mountains." *Journal of Hellenic Studies* 112: 1–15.

Carney, Thomas F.
1975   *The Shape of the Past: Models and Antiquity.*
               Lawrence, Kan.: Coronado.

Charles, R. H.
1920   *An Exegetical and Critical Commentary on the
               Book of Revelation.* 2 vols. Edinburgh: Clark.

Chevalier, Jacques M.
1997   *A Postmodern Revelation: Signs of Astrology and
               the Apocalypse.* Toronto: Univ. of Toronto Press.

Chyutin, Michael
1994   "The New Jerusalem: Ideal City." *Dead Sea Dis-
               coveries* 1: 71–97.

Coleman, John A.
1999   "The Bible and Sociology: 1998 Paul Hanly Fur-
               fey Lecture." *Sociology of Religion* 60: 125–148.

Collins, John J. (ed.)
1979   *Apocalypse: The Morphology of a Genre.* Semeia
               14. Missoula: Society of Biblical Literature.

Corbier, Mireille
1991   "City, Territory and Taxation." In *City and Coun-
               try in the Ancient World,* edited by John Rich and
               Andrew Wallace-Hadrill, 211–239. New York and
               London: Routledge.

Cornell, Timothy J.
1991   "Rome: The History of an Anachronism." In *City
               States in Classical Antiquity and Medieval Italy,*
               edited by Anthony Molho, Kurt Raaflaub, and Julia
               Emlen, 53–69. Ann Arbor: Univ. of Michigan Press.

Cumont, Franz.
1960   *Astrology and Religion Among the Greeks and the
               Romans.* 1912. New York: Dover Publications.

1919   "Zodiacus." In *Dictionnaire des antiquités grec-
               ques et romaines V,* edited by C. Darembert and E.
               Saglio, 1046–1062. Paris: Hachette.

Cumont, Franz et al. (eds.)
1898–1953   *Catalogus Codicum Astrologicorum Graecorum.*
               12 vols. Brussels: Lamertin.

Daniélou, Jean
1964   *The Theology of Jewish Christianity.* Chicago:
               Regnery.

De Long, J. Bradford, and Andrei Shleifer
1993   "Princes and Merchants: European City Growth
               Before the Industrial Revolution." *Journal of Law
               and Economics* 36: 671.

De Tarragon, Jean-Michel.
1995   "Witchcraft, Magic and Divination in Canaan and
               Ancient Israel." In *Civilizations of the Ancient Near
               East,* edited by Jack M. Sasson, 3:2071–2081.
               New York: Scribner.

Duncan-Jones, Richard
1982   *The Economy of the Roman Empire: Quantitative
               Studies.* 2nd ed. Cambridge: Cambridge Univ. Press.

Ebner, Michael H., and Stuart M. Blumin, Lynn Hollen Lees, Bruce M.
Stave, Samuel P. Hays
1993   "Samuel P. Hays and the Social Analysis of the City:
               A Symposium." *Journal of Urban History* 19: 85.

Eder, Walter
1991   "Who Rules? Power and Participation in Athens
               and Rome." In *City States in Classical Antiquity
               and Medieval Italy,* edited by Anthony Molho,
               Kurt Raaflaub, and Julia Emlen, 169–196. Ann
               Arbor: Univ. of Michigan Press.

Elliott, John H.
1990   *A Home for the Homeless: A Social-Scientific Criti-
               cism of 1 Peter, Its Situation and Strategy, with a
               New Introduction.* Rev. ed. Minneapolis: Fortress.

Festugière, André-J.
1950   *La Révélation d'Hermès Trismégiste.* Vol. 1, *L'As-
               trologie de les sciences occultes.* Paris: Gabalda.

Figueira, Thomas J.
1991   "A Typology of Social Conflict in Greek Poleis."
               In *City States in Classical Antiquity and Medieval
               Italy,* edited by Anthony Molho, Kurt Raaflaub,
               and Julia Emlen, 289–308. Ann Arbor: Univ. of
               Michigan Press.

Finley, M. I.
1977   "The Ancient City: From Fustel de Coulanges to
                        Max Weber and Beyond." *CSSH* 19: 305–327.

Fisher, L. R.
1963   "The Temple Quarter." *Journal of Semitic Studies*
                        8: 34–41.

Flanagan, James G.
1989   "Hierarchy in Simple 'Egalitarian' Societies." *An-
                        nual Review of Anthropology* 18: 245–266.

Flusser, David
1988   *Judaism and the Origins of Christianity.* Jerusa-
                        lem: Magnes.

Ford, Josephine Massyngberde
1975   *Revelation.* The Anchor Bible. Garden City, N.Y.:
                        Doubleday.

Frier, Bruce W.
1983   "Urban Praetors and Rural Violence: The Legal
                        Background of Cicero's Pro Caecina." *TAPA* 113:
                        221–241.

Giovannini, Adalberto
1991   "Symbols and Rituals in Classical Athens." In *City
                        States in Classical Antiquity and Medieval Italy,*
                        edited by Anthony Molho, Kurt Raaflaub, and Julia
                        Emlen, 459–478. Ann Arbor: Univ. of Michigan
                        Press.

Goetz, Albrecht (trans.)
1969   "Hittite Rituals, Incantations, and Descriptions of
                        Festivals." In *Ancient Near Eastern Texts Relat-
                        ing to the Old Testament,* 3rd. ed., edited by J. B.
                        Pritchard, 346–361. Princeton: Princeton Univ.
                        Press.

Golding, Naomi
1975   "Plato as City Planner." *Arethusa* 8: 359–371.

Greer, Rowan A.
1986   "Alien Citizens: A Marvellous Paradox." In *Civi-
                        tas: Religious Interpretations of the City,* edited by
                        Peter S. Hawkins, 39–56. Atlanta: Scholars Press.

Gregory, Timothy E.
1983   "Urban Violence in Late Antiquity." In *Aspects of
                Greco-Roman Urbanism: Essays on the Classical
                City,* edited by Ronald T. Marchese, 138–161.
                BAR International Series 188. Oxford: BAR.

Grelot, Pierre
1958   "La Géographie mythique d'Hénoch et ses source
                orientales." *Revue Biblique* 65: 33–69.

Gruen, Erich S.
1991   "The Exercise of Power in the Roman Republic."
                In *City States in Classical Antiquity and Medieval
                Italy,* edited by Anthony Molho, Kurt Raaflaub,
                and Julia Emlen, 251–268. Ann Arbor: Univ. of
                Michigan Press.

Gundel, Wilhelm
1936a   *Dekane und Dekansternbilder: Ein Beitrag zur
                Geschichte der Sternbilder der Kulturvölker. Mit
                einer Untersuchung über die Ägyptischen Stern-
                bilder und Gottheiten der Dekane von S. Schott.* Stu-
                dien der Bibliothek Warburg 19. Glückstadt and
                Hamburg: J. J. Augustin.

1936b   *Neue astrologische Texte des Hermes Trismegis-
                tos: Funde und Forschungen auf dem Gebiet der
                antiken Astronomie und Astrologie.* Abhandlun-
                gen der Bayerischen Akademie der Wissenschaf-
                ten. Philosophisch-historische Abteilung, n.F. 12.
                Munich: Verlag der Bayerischen Akademie der
                Wissenschaften.

1950   "Astronomie." In *Reallexikon für Antike und Chris-
                tentum,* 1:817–831. Stuttgart: Hiersmann.

Halliday, Michael A. K.
1978   *Language as Social Semiotic: The Social Interpre-
                tation of Language and Meaning.* Baltimore: Uni-
                versity Park Press.

Hansen, Mogens Herman and Kurt Raaflaub (eds.)
1995   *Studies in the Ancient Greek Polis.* Historia: Einzel-
                schriften 95. Stuttgart: Steiner.

Hanson, K. C.
1994[95]   "Transformed on the Mountain: Ritual Analysis
                  and the Gospel of Matthew." *Semeia* 67: 147–170.

Hartigan, Karelisa V.
1978   "The Ancient City: Its Concept and Expression."
                 Helios 6/2: 45–49.

Hays, Samuel P.
1993   "From the History of the City to the History of Ur-
                 banized Society." *Journal of Urban History* 19:
                 3–25.

Hölscher, Tonio
1991   "The City of Athens: Space, Symbol, Structure."
                 In *City States in Classical Antiquity and Medieval
                 Italy,* edited by Anthony Molho, Kurt Raaflaub,
                 and Julia Emlen, 355–380. Ann Arbor: Univ. of
                 Michigan Press.

Hopkins, Keith
1991   "From Violence to Blessing: Symbols and Rituals
                 in Ancient Rome." In *City States in Classical An-
                 tiquity,* edited by Anthony Molho, Kurt Raaflaub,
                 and Julia Emlen, 479–498. Ann Arbor: Univ. of
                 Michigan Press.

Hsu, Francis L. K.
1983   *Rugged Individualism Reconsidered: Essays in
                 Psychological Anthropology.* Knoxville: Univ. of
                 Tennessee Press.

Lewellen, Ted C.
1983   *Political Anthropology: An Introduction.* South
                 Hadley, Mass.: Bergin and Garvey.

Liddell, Henry, and Robert Scott
1997   *An Intermediate Greek-English Lexicon.* 1889.
                 Oxford: Clarendon Press.

Ling, Roger
1990   "A Stranger in Town: Finding the Way in an An-
                 cient City." *Greece and Rome* 37: 204–214.

Loraux, Nicole
1991   "Reflections of the Greek City on Unity and Divi-
                 sion." In *City States in Classical Antiquity and*

Medieval Italy, edited by Anthony Molho, Kurt Raaflaub, and Julia Emlen, 33–51. Ann Arbor: Univ. of Michigan Press.

Malina, Bruce J.

1983   "The Social Sciences and Biblical Interpretation." *Interpretation* 37 (1982): 229–242; reprinted in *The Bible and Liberation,* edited by Norman K. Gottwald, 11–25. Maryknoll: Orbis.

1983   "Why Interpret the Bible with the Social Sciences?" *American Baptist Quarterly* 2: 119–133.

1986   "Religion in the World of Paul: A Preliminary Sketch." *Biblical Theology Bulletin* 16: 92–101.

1991   "Interpretation: Reading, Abduction, Metaphor." In *The Bible and the Politics of Exegesis: Essays in Honor of Norman K. Gottwald on His Sixty-Fifth Birthday,* edited by David Jobling, Peggy L. Day, and Gerald T. Sheppard, 253–266. Cleveland: Pilgrim Press.

1992   "Is There a Circum-Mediterranean Person: Looking for Stereotypes." *Biblical Theology Bulletin* 22: 66–87.

1993a   "Apocalyptic and Territoriality." In *Early Christianity in Context: Monuments and Documents. Essays in Honour of Emmanuel Testa,* edited by Frederic Manns and Eugenio Alliata, 369–380. Jerusalem: Franciscan Printing Press.

1993b   *The New Testament World: Insights from Cultural Anthropology.* Rev. ed. Louisville: Knox/Westminster.

1994   "Religion in the Imagined New Testament World: More Social Science Lenses." *Scriptura* 51: 1–26.

1995   *On the Genre and Message of Revelation: Star Visions and Sky Journeys.* Peabody, Mass.: Hendrickson.

1996a   "Reading Theory Perspectives." In *The Social World of Jesus and the Gospels,* 3–31. London and New York: Routledge.

1996b   "Christ and Time: Swiss or Mediterranean." In *The
                 Social World of Jesus and the Gospels,* 179–214.
                 London and New York: Routledge.

1996c   "Social Scientific Criticism and Rhetorical Criti-
                 cism: Why Won't Romanticism Leave Us Alone?"
                 In *Rhetoric, Scripture and Theology: Essays from
                 the 1994 Pretoria Conference,* edited by Stanley
                 E. Porter and Thomas H. Olbricht, 71–101. *JSNT*
                 Suppl. Sheffield: Sheffield Academic Press.

1997   "Jesus as Astral Prophet." *Biblical Theology Bul-
                 letin* 27: 83–98.

1998   "How a Cosmic Lamb Marries: The Image of the
                 Wedding of the Lamb (Rev 19:7ff)." *Biblical The-
                 ology Bulletin* 28: 75–83.

2000a   "Everyday Christian Experience: Social Levels,
                 Morals and Daily Life." In *Encyclopedia of the
                 Early Christian World,* edited by Philip F. Esler.
                 London and New York: Routledge.

2000b   *The Social Gospel of Jesus: The Kingdom of God in
                 Mediterranean Perspective.* Minneapolis: Fortress.

Malina, Bruce J., and Jerome H. Neyrey
1991   "First-Century Personality: Dyadic, Not Individ-
                 ual." In *The Social World of Luke-Acts: Models for
                 Interpretation,* edited by Jerome H. Neyrey, 67–96.
                 Peabody, Mass.: Hendrickson.

1996   *Portraits of Paul: An Archaeology of Ancient Per-
                 sonality.* Louisville: Westminster/John Knox.

Malina, Bruce J., and John J. Pilch
2000   *Social Science Commentary on the Book of Reve-
                 lation.* Minneapolis: Fortress.

Marchese, Ronald T. (ed.)
1983   *Aspects of Greco-Roman Urbanism: Essays on the
                 Classical City.* BAR International Series 188. Ox-
                 ford: BAR.

Mellaart, James
1975   "The Origins and Development of Cities in the
                 Near East." In *Janus: Essays in Ancient and Mod-*

ern Studies, edited by Louis L. Orlin, 5–22. Ann
Arbor: Univ. of Michigan Press.

Metzger, Martin
1996   "Himmlisches Jerusalem und Tempelarchitektur:
Ein Beitrag zum Verständnis von Apokalypse
21,16f." In *Gemeinschaft am Evengelium: Fest-
schrift für Wiard Popkes zum 60. Geburtstag,* edited
by Edwin Brandt, Paul S. Fiddes, and Joachim
Molthagen, 97–126. Leipzig: Evangelische Ver-
lagsanstalt.

Milik, Józef T., with Matthew Black
1976   *The Books of Enoch: Aramaic Fragments from
Qumran Cave 4.* Oxford: Clarendon.

Millar, Fergus
1983   "Empire and City, Augustus to Julian: Obligations, Excuses and Status." *Journal of Roman Studies* 73: 76–96.

Miller, Doris S.
1983   "Bostra in Arabia: Nabatean and Roman City of
the Near East." In *Aspects of Greco-Roman Urbanism: Essays on the Classical City,* edited by
Ronald T. Marchese, 110–137. BAR International
Series 188. Oxford: BAR.

Molho, Anthony, Kurt Raaflaub, and Julia Emlen (eds.)
1991   *City States in Classical Antiquity and Medieval
Italy.* Ann Arbor: Univ. of Michigan Press.

Moore, Michael S.
1982   "Jesus Christ: 'Superstar' Revelation xxii 16b."
Novum Testamentum 24: 82–91.

Muse, Robert L.
1996   *The Book of Revelation: An Annotated Bibliography.* New York: Garland.

Musiolek, Peter
1978   "Zur Problematik der Stadt im Hellenismus." *Klio*
60: 93–100.

Needham, Joseph
1981   "Time and Knowledge in China and the West." In
The Voices of Time: A Cooperative Survey of Man's

Views of Time as Expressed by the Sciences and the Humanities, 2nd ed., edited by J. T. Fraser, 92–135. Amherst: Univ. of Massachusetts Press.

Nippel, Wilfried
1991   "Max Weber's 'The City' Revisited." In *City States in Classical Antiquity and Medieval Italy,* edited by Anthony Molho, Kurt Raaflaub, and Julia Emlen, 19–30. Ann Arbor: Univ. of Michigan Press.

Nock, A., and A. Festugière (eds. and trans.)
1946   *Corpus Hermeticum.* 4 vols. Paris: Les-Belles Lettres.

Nutini, Hugo G.
1972   "The Latin American City: A Cultural-Historical Approach." In *The Anthropology of Urban Environments,* edited by Thomas Weaver and Douglas White, 89–95. Society of Applied Anthropology Monograph Series 11. Washington: Society for Applied Anthropology.

Oakman, Douglas E.
1991   "The Countryside in Luke-Acts." In *The Social World of Luke-Acts: Models for Interpretation,* edited by Jerome H. Neyrey, 151–179. Peabody, Mass.: Hendrickson.

Orlin, Louis L.
1975   "Ancient Near Eastern Cities: Form, Function and Idea." In *Janus: Essays in Ancient and Modern Studies,* edited by Louis L. Orlin, 25–54. Ann Arbor: Univ. of Michigan Press.

Orr, David G.
1983   "The Roman City: A Philosophical and Cultural Summa." In *Aspects of Greco-Roman Urbanism: Essays on the Classical City,* edited by Ronald T. Marchese, 93–109. BAR International Series 188. Oxford: BAR.

Owens, E. J.
1991   *The City in the Greek and Roman World.* New York and London: Routledge.

Patterson, J. R.
1992   "The City of Rome: From Republic to Empire."
                        Journal of Roman Studies 82: 186–215.

Pilch, John J.
1993   "Visions in Revelation and Alternate Conscious-
                        ness: A Perspective from Cultural Anthropology."
                        Listening 28: 231–244.

1994   "Secrecy in the Mediterranean World: An Anthro-
                        pological Perspective." *Biblical Theology Bulletin*
                        24: 151–157.

1995   "The Transfiguration of Jesus: An Experience of
                        Alternate Reality." In *Modelling Early Christian-
                        ity: Social-scientific Studies of the New Testament
                        in its Context,* edited by Philip F. Esler, 47–64.
                        London and New York: Routledge.

1996   "Altered States of Consciousness: A 'Kitbashed'
                        Model." *Biblical Theology Bulletin* 26: 133–138.

Potter, David
1992   "Empty Areas and Roman Frontier Policy." *AJPh*
                        113: 269–274.

Prickett, Stephen
1996   *Origins of Narrative: The Romantic Appropriation
                        of the Bible.* Cambridge: Cambridge Univ. Press.

Raaflaub, Kurt
1991   "City-State, Territory and Empire in Classical An-
                        tiquity." In *City States in Classical Antiquity and
                        Medieval Italy,* edited by Anthony Molho, Kurt
                        Raaflaub, and Julia Emlen, 565–588. Ann Arbor:
                        Univ. of Michigan Press.

Ramage, Edwin S.
1983   "Urban Problems in Ancient Rome." In *Aspects of
                        Greco-Roman Urbanism: Essays on the Classical
                        City,* edited by Ronald T. Marchese, 61–92. BAR
                        International Series 188. Oxford: BAR.

Randsborg, Klaus
1989   "The Demise of Antiquity: Europe and the Medi-
                        terranean in the First Millennium AD." *Annual
                        Review of Anthropology* 19: 227–244.

Richardson, L., Jr.
1991   "Urban Development in Ancient Rome and the Impact of Empire." In *City States in Classical Antiquity and Medieval Italy,* edited by Anthony Molho, Kurt Raaflaub, and Julia Emlen, 381–402. Ann Arbor: Univ. of Michigan Press.

Rohrbaugh, Richard L.
1991a   "The Pre-industrial City in Luke-Acts: Urban Social Relations." In *The Social World of Luke-Acts: Models for Interpretation,* edited by Jerome H. Neyrey, 125–149. Peabody, Mass.: Hendrickson.

1991b   "The City in the Second Testament." *Biblical Theology Bulletin* 21: 67–75.

1996   "The Preindustrial City." In *The Social Sciences and New Testament Interpretation,* edited by Richard L. Rohrbaugh, 107–125. Peabody, Mass.: Hendrickson.

Rordorf, Willi
1968   *Sunday: The History of the Day of Rest and Worship in the Earliest Centuries of the Christian Church.* Philadelphia: Westminster.

Rosenhan, D. L.
1973   "On Being Sane in Insane Places." *Science* 179: 250–258.

Runia, David T.
1989   "Polis and Megalopolis: Philo and the Founding of Alexandria." *Mnemosyne* 42: 398–412.

Sack, Robert David
1986   *Human Territoriality: Its Theory and History.* Cambridge Studies in Historical Geography. Cambridge: Cambridge Univ. Press.

Sanford, A. J., and S. C. Garrod
1981   *Understanding Written Language: Explorations of Comprehension Beyond the Sentence.* New York: Wiley.

Sanjek, Roger
1990   "Urban Anthropology in the 1980's: A World View." *Annual Review of Anthropology* 19: 151–186.

Santos Velasco, Juan A.
1994   "City and State in Pre-Roman Spain: The Ex-
            ample of Ilici." *Antiquity* 68: 289–299.

Scott, Alan
1991   *Origen and the Life of the Stars: A History of an
            Idea.* Oxford: Clarendon.

Scully, Stephen
1981   "The Polis in Homer: A Definition and Interpreta-
            tion." *Ramus* 10: 1–34.

1990   *Homer and the Sacred City.* Ithaca, N.Y.: Cornell
            Univ. Press.

Sim, Unyong
1996   *Das himmlische Jerusalem in Apk 21,1–22,5 im
            Kontext biblisch-jüdischer Tradition und antiken
            Städtebaus.* Bochumer Altertumswissenschaft-
            liches Colloquium 25. Trier: WVT.

Smith, Morton
1971   "Prolegomena to a Discussion of Aretalogies, Di-
            vine Men, the Gospels and Jesus." *Journal of Bib-
            lical Literature* 90: 174–199.

1952   "The Common Theology of the Ancient Near East."
            Journal of Biblical Literature 71: 135–147.

1983   "On the History of Apokalypto and Apokalypsis."
            In *Apocalypticism in the Mediterranean World
            and the Near East,* edited by David Helholm, 9–20.
            Tübingen: Mohr.

Söllner, Peter
1998   *Jerusalem, die hochgebaute Stadt: Eschatologis-
            ches und Himmlisches Jerusalem im Frühjudentum
            und im frühen Christentum.* TANZ 25. Tübingen:
            Francke Verlag.

Southall, Aidan
1998   *The City in Time and Space.* Cambridge: Cam-
            bridge Univ. Press.

Stambaugh, John E.
1973–74   "The Idea of the City: Three Views of Athens." *CJ*
            69: 309–321.

Tertullian
1957   *Against Marcion*. Edited by A. Roberts and J.
                     Donaldson. *The Ante-Nicene Fathers*. Vol. 3. Grand
                     Rapids: Wm. B. Eerdmans.

Thornton, M. K.
1986   "Julio-Claudian Building Programs: Eat, Drink,
                     and Be Merry." *Historia* 35: 28–44.

Van der Toorn, Karel
1995   "Theology, Priests, and Worship in Canaan and
                     Ancient Israel." In *Civilizations of the Ancient
                     Near East*, edited by Jack M. Sasson, 3:2043–2058.
                     New York: Scribner.

Von Rad, Gerhard
1966   "The City on the Hill." In *The Problem of the
                     Hexateuch and Other Essays*, 232–242. New York:
                     McGraw-Hill.

Wallace-Hadrill, Andrew
1991   "Elites and Trade in the Roman Town." In *City
                     and Country in the Ancient World*, edited by John
                     Rich and Andrew Wallace-Hadrill, 241–272. New
                     York and London: Routledge.

Weaver, Thomas, and Douglas White
1972   "Anthropological Approaches to Urban and Com-
                     plex Society." In *The Anthropology of Urban En-
                     vironments*, edited by Thomas Weaver and Douglas
                     White, 109–125. Society of Applied Anthropol-
                     ogy Monograph Series 11. Washington: Society
                     for Applied Anthropology.

Wengst, Klaus
1994   "Babylon the Great and the New Jerusalem: The
                     Visionary View of Political Reality in the Revela-
                     tion of John." In *Politics and Theopolitics in the
                     Bible and Postbiblical Literature*, edited by Hen-
                     ning Graf Reventlow, Yair Hoffman, and Ben-
                     jamin Uffenheimer, 189–202. JSOT, Suppl. 171.
                     Sheffield: Sheffield Academic Press.

White, Douglas, and Thomas Weaver
1972   "Sociological Contributions to an Urban Anthro-
                     pology." In *The Anthropology of Urban Environ-*

ments, edited by Thomas Weaver and Douglas White, 97–107. Society of Applied Anthropology Monograph Series 11. Washington: Society for Applied Anthropology.

Whitehead, David
1991

"Norms of Citizenship in Ancient Greece." In *City States in Classical Antiquity and Medieval Italy,* edited by Anthony Molho, Kurt Raaflaub, and Julia Emlen, 135–154. Ann Arbor: Univ. of Michigan Press.

Wiggermann, F. A. M.
1995

"Theologies, Priests, and Worship in Ancient Mesopotamia." In *Civilizations of the Ancient Near East,* edited by Jack M. Sasson, 3:1857–1870. New York: Scribner.

Wiseman, T. P.
1992

"Reading the City: History, Poetry, and the Topography of Rome." *Classical Quarterly* 69: 94–96.

Yadin, Yigael
1983

The Temple Scroll. 2 vols. Jerusalem: Israel Exploration Society.

Index